PRAI

MW00813080

Instructions Not Included:

A Pediatrician's Prescription for Raising the Best Kids on the Block

"Sure, the child needs a pediatrician, but so does the parent, along with a comprehensive set of operating instructions! From predicting your child's growth and deciding on vaccinations, to helping your teen navigate sexuality, plus every stage in between, Dr. Berkowitz shares nuggets of wisdom gleaned from decades of medical and parental experience. Part memoir, part child-rearing handbook, the thoughtfulness and warmth of this seasoned, caring physician shines through on every page."

~ MARY JANE CLARK,
New York Times bestselling author and parent of two

"Bravo! Practical advice and pithy insight from the lens of a seasoned Pediatrician. Dr. Berkowitz captures a unique blend of the personal with the professional whereby decades of 'medical wisdom' meets the 'kitchen table'. He takes you on a journey across development. With a steady hand and comforting voice, he illustrates 'on the job training'; guiding parents through the murky waters with calm aplomb. His humanism stands out – both with patients and his self-view. I'm a fan."

~ JUSTIN K. PALTROWITZ, MD,
Child, Adolescent, and Adult Psychiatry

"In his compelling, informative, and entertaining retrospective on 40 years of immersion in the care of infants, children, adolescents, and their caregivers, Dr. Berkowitz imparts clinical pearls, life lessons, and invaluable tips in equal doses. He does so with lively writing, humor, and humility. He smoothly intertwines his own development as child, callow youth, budding student, emerging doctor, doting father (and husband) with what he sees in the consulting room day-in, day out. With this book that patients, parents, and practitioners both young and seasoned, will find invaluable, Dr. Berkowitz joins the ranks of the Spocks, Brazeltons, and Illingworths who successfully extended their healing reach beyond those lucky enough to have felt their care and attention in person."

– THOMAS HOFFMAN, MD,
Pediatrician, Psychoanalyst, and Behavioral Scientist

"Over fifteen years ago my older son was born with a defect in his heart. Understandably, my husband and I were nervous and upset. I had heard about how Dr. Berkowitz had kept my mother-in-law calm while raising three kids, my husband being the oldest. When I met Dr. Berkowitz for the first time, I knew instantly my son (and I) was in the best hands possible. Calm, warm, professional and approachable, Dr. Berkowitz has helped us through five major surgeries (between my two boys) and countless visits and illnesses. With his sense of humor, knowledge and true caring for both children and adults, my older son is now 5 feet 10 inches tall and thriving. We thank Dr. Berkowitz every day not only for keeping us calm, but also for now successfully taking care of two generations of our family. There is no better person to write about pediatric medicine. This book is a perfect balance of practical information presented in a humorous way that helps every person understand the joys and challenges of raising a child – which is exactly how Dr. Berkowitz practices medicine every day of his life."

– AMY ZUCKERMAN,
mother of a patient

"As a pediatrician and department chair, I thoroughly enjoyed reading Dr. Berkowitz's personal text which highlights the experience that most of us had while in medical school, post graduate residency and in our practices. It is a text which will demonstrate the high degree of professionalism, huge scope of knowledge and most importantly the dedication required to be a competent pediatrician.

I recommend this text with enthusiasm for those medical students who are interested in primary care and for those future pediatricians who want to know what is possible in terms of personal satisfaction and career enjoyment."

~ LEONARD J. NEWMAN MD,
Professor and Chairman, New York Medical College

Instructions Not Included

A PARENTING GUIDE AND MEDICAL MEMOIR

Instructions Not Included

*A Pediatrician's Prescription for Raising
the Best Kids on the Block*

IRWIN H. BERKOWITZ, MD

Instructions Not Included
© 2014 Irwin H. Berkowitz, MD
www.irwinhberkowitzmd.com

All rights reserved worldwide. No part of this publication may be reproduced, distributed, or transmitted in any form or by any means, electronic or mechanical, including photocopy, recording, or any information storage and retrieval system, without written permission from the author except in the case of brief quotations, embodied in critical reviews and certain other noncommercial uses permitted by copyright law.

Some names and identifying details have been changed to protect the privacy of individuals. This book is not intended as a substitute relating to your child's health particularly with respect to any symptoms that may require diagnosis or medical attention.

Permission granted on page XV: Headline: Robert Manzi, Ridgefield Doctor; Date: June 22, 2013; Byline: Lindy Washburn; Source: © 2013 Lindy Washburn / Northjersey.com.

Credit for quote on page 67: *The Death of Santini: The Story of a Father and His Son*, Pat Conroy, Published by Nan A. Talese / Doubleday, a division of Random House LLC, New York.

Publisher's Cataloging-in-Publication Data

Berkowitz, Irwin H.
    Instructions not included : a pediatrician's prescription
for raising the best kids on the block / Irwin H. Berkowitz.
    pages cm
    ISBN: 978-0-9960785-1-1 (pbk.)
    ISBN: 978-0-9960785-2-8 (e-book)
    1. Parenting. 2. Parenthood. 3. Pediatricians—
Biography. 4. Child development.   I. Title.
HQ755.8 .B4765 2014
649—dc23
                        2014937008

Cover design, book design and production by Bobbi Benson, Wild Ginger Press.
www.wildgingerpress.com

For Kathleen

CONTENTS

Me and my protégé.

PREFACE

Kernels and Blossoms

THIS WORK BLOSSOMED from a single kernel of advice imparted to me more than 40 years ago by a wise pediatrician concerning whether infants and toddlers could seriously injure themselves in everyday falls. (It's extremely unlikely, but more about that later.) Over the decades since, mentors and colleagues have passed on to me many more seeds of knowledge. I've also had wonderful patients who've taught me through their illnesses and who've tested my thinking with their challenging questions. All this plus plenty of reading has fertilized those early grains of knowledge and coaxed them to bloom into my very own set of ideas about child-rearing. I've shared those ideas with my patients in turn, trying always to select whichever blossoms of wisdom seemed most helpful for managing a particular medical situation. Now, I'm ready to share that philosophy of care with a wider audience.

My writing has progressed in fits and starts. There were months where I wrote nothing and focused instead on accumulating ideas and formulating concepts before picking this work back up and beginning to write again. And the more I wrote, the more ideas revealed themselves.

I taught pediatric residents for five years at the start of my career, and for the past 15 years, I've taught medical students. I've also guided mothers, fathers and patients throughout my entire career, and over the course of these interactions, I've tried to perfect my communication style so that it is clear, concise and holds the listener's attention. Now, as I wind down in my career, I hope to share some of the wisdom that I've worked so hard to obtain with young parents and pediatric physicians as well as with healthcare providers-in-training.

I've tried to be a compassionate physician who listens to his patients carefully, shows concern for their well-being, and does what is proper no matter what. Just the other day I spent 20 minutes explaining to a mom that her child didn't need antibiotics for his fever. She wasn't very happy with me. The easiest thing would have been to just give her the prescription rather than spend time and energy explaining to her the danger and inappropriateness of the misuse and overuse of antibiotics. But it wouldn't have been the right thing.

In the following pages, I'll describe my own personal journey to becoming a pediatrician, and then I invite you to join me on a guided tour through childhood, as experienced from the perspective of both child and parent. Sadly, there is no such thing as a Paradigm of Proper Parenting Wisdom. What I've assembled instead is a compendium of commonsense child-rearing tips culled from many years of caring for children and their parents.

Not long ago, we hired a new pediatrician for our practice, Rebecca, who had heard positive things about us from a former patient, Amy. After finishing her residency, Rebecca had worked at a clinic run by the medical school. When she mentioned to a resident at the clinic that she'd applied to work with us, the resident delighted her with recollections of childhood visits to our office. Amy recounted how much she'd enjoyed these visits as a child, teenager and young adult, and how this positive experience had inspired her to become a doctor. It is one of the great pleasures of being a pediatrician continuously working in the same practice to witness the development of an infant into a child, adult and even sometimes a parent. It is particularly rewarding to think that, in some way, the care and knowledge I imparted to a patient or his parent might have pointed him or her in a positive direction.

Recently, a beloved physician, Robert Manzi, MD, died after struggling with multiple medical problems. He was eulogized in a regional newspaper, *The Bergen Record*, with the following words: "Dr. Manzi loved to get his patients laughing with his down-to-earth humor … [He] prided himself on practicing medicine the old-fashioned way – asking careful questions, taking a thorough history, and relying on years of experience rather than a printout of test results."

I, too, aspire to these goals. I hope that you as a reader benefit in some way from my efforts to impart some of the wisdom I've acquired during my years in practice. One of the ways I judge the value of a lesson is if I come away from it with at least one fact or idea that changes the way I think or act. I invite you to judge me, and this work, by the same measure.

D day-1 in front of Chestnut Ridge Pediatrics
with Kathleen and my parents.

ACKNOWLEDGMENT

THIS BOOK IS DEDICATED to my dear wife, Kathleen, who in turn painstakingly dedicated her life to our children and to our family and shared me with my other calling. This allowed me the opportunity to devote what was perhaps an unfair amount of time and energy to my profession. She has been a wonderful mother and wife.

I also want to thank my children, who have taught me so much about being a father and a pediatrician. They've humbled me. They've also shown me that child-rearing doesn't always follow the rulebook, and that our emotions can sometimes affect our better judgment.

My cousin, French children's book author Susie Morgenstern, read the manuscript in its embryonic stages and encouraged me to continue writing because she saw value in what I was trying to do. I want to thank Erin J. Bernard, my editor, who enthusiastically embraced my idea and my imperfect attempts at writing, fine-tuning the manuscript into a cohesive work. Bobbi Benson has assisted me with all of the details involved with the publishing and marketing of my book.

I am grateful to all of my teachers, who encouraged my love of learning. I appreciate all of my mentors in medicine who happily shared their wisdom and enthusiasm for the healing profession with me. I also wish to thank my patients and their parents for having the confidence in me to allow me to care for them. Through their illnesses and their concerns, they have also taught me.

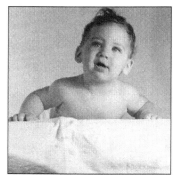

Contemplating my future profession.

The graduate.

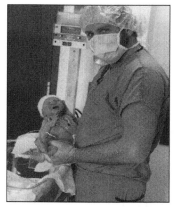

*The Young Doctor smiling under his
mask at the joy of a new birth.*

Part One

How to Make a Pediatrician

SOMETIMES I'M ASKED how long I've been a practicing pediatrician. After 40 years, though, I'm not really practicing at all; I've got this gig down pat.

Over four decades, I've performed approximately 200,000 examinations on around 30,000 patients. I've seen about 20,000 episodes of sore throat and I've treated 10,000 cases of asthma visits and at least 5000 ear infections. I've also encountered my share of rare diseases – those with incidences of one case per 50,000 or fewer – in my office and during rotations through specialty centers.

Every day as a pediatrician brings new triumphs and new challenges. Even the same disease is different each time I encounter it because new people are involved. But always, being a pediatrician involves caring for at least two patients: the child, and one or both parents.

A pediatrician's job is not only to prevent and cure disease, but also to educate families and to help them cope with truly serious medical issues as well as those conditions the family perceives to be serious even though, in reality, they aren't. Reassuring parents that these situations aren't life-threatening and providing parents the tools to deal with them allows both my patients and their parents to develop a healthy attitude toward sickness. Teaching parents about danger signs allows them to step back and see illnesses in a more objective manner. This knowledge gives them a sense of control, which provides a degree of calm. After all, feeling out of control is one of the scariest emotions a human being can face, and the wise counsel of an understanding physician can go a long way toward alleviating uncertainty.

These days I am treating the children of my patients, and I recently learned of the birth of my first grandpatient. D.J. (Doug Junior) was born in spring 2013, weighing in at 6 pounds, 10 ounces. His father, Doug, and grandmother Debbie are both prior patients. Will I live to welcome a great-grandpatient? Time will tell.

ONE

My Journey
to Medical School

DOCTORS HAVE BEEN MAKING HOUSE CALLS to the living rooms of American families for decades by way of popular medical television dramas, but how well do they capture the reality of being a physician? I did watch *Ben Casey*, *Dr. Kildare* and *Marcus Welby, M.D.*, on TV in the '60s and '70s, but they were not the inspiration for my path toward medicine, and I certainly didn't see them as role models. These shows glamorize and sometimes comically misrepresent the life of an MD.

Here's what I remember about real-life doctors from my childhood: Dr. Friedlander, my family physician, assaulting me with a shot of penicillin – not at all inspiring. I had only a vague concept of what a physician did. What I did have was a love of learning and a desire to help people.

In recent years, the now-retired TV series *House* purported to depict the life of an unorthodox, hospital-based physician who was also struggling with a painkiller addiction. All I can say is that if I made as many diagnostic errors as he made in just one show before he came to the right conclusion, my medical license would have been rescinded long ago.

To Be or not to Be: Deciding on a Life in Medicine

What ultimately made me want to become a physician? To tell you the truth, I really don't know. My earliest recollections go back to the time when I was about 4 years old, and the recent beneficiary of a baby brother. I remember that I had a book titled *Doctor Dan the Bandage Man*, whose most striking characteristic was a sheet of bandages attached to its back cover. Was that the source of my epiphany? Being the first-born son of first-generation Jewish-American parents, a career in medicine might have been prescribed for me in one of the holy books. An old, not-so-politically correct joke asks, "When does a Jewish fetus become viable?"

The answer: "After it graduates medical school."

It may also have been genetics. Three of my four older cousins on the paternal side became either physicians or dentists. Whatever the genesis, I was interested in medicine from a young age. Then seventh grade arrived. I was in a program called "2-Year SP (Special Progress)," in which the seventh through ninth grades were combined into two years. In retrospect, for me, SP should have stood for "Stupid Plan," as I had entered kindergarten at 4-and-a-half years old because of the birthday cutoff and was therefore destined to start college before I even reached puberty.

During a school assembly that year, we watched a film called something along the lines of *I Am a Doctor*. The film showed one of the first open-heart surgeries, including a scene in which the chest was cracked open to reveal the bloody, beating heart. This was too much for my 11-year old brain. I covered my head to keep my brain from exploding, and there went my plans for becoming a doctor.

What was my new career path to be? It so happened that my local public high school was not very good, so I had to choose between a private religious high school and one of the specialized New York City high schools that required an entrance exam. I settled on my second career path – architect or engineer – and decided to attend Brooklyn Technical High School. This school, which was comprised of 6000 boys, specialized in engineering. Tech, as it was called, was a daunting, yellow-brick building rising 11 stories and culminating with a screened-in roof, used as an outdoor gym. It soared above a neighborhood of shabby row houses, one step above a slum. I traveled an hour and a half by bus and train each way. The school's strengths were in math and science but I had some of the most wonderful history and language teachers there. I briefly entertained the idea of becoming a lawyer after being inspired by Mr. Kahn, a history teacher who brought history into the present for me. As I struggled through mechanical and architectural drawing, I realized I was spatially challenged. I also realized that engineering didn't inspire me. There went my next two career choices. In Tech, physics was mandatory and biology was optional. I decided to confront my demons and take biology in my senior year to see if I had what it took to handle dissection.

In the meantime, I needed to pick a college. So I decided on my next career: accounting. I applied to Baruch College of the City College of New York. At the same time I was attending orientation at Baruch College, I was successfully navigating biology back at Tech, even ably dissecting a dead frog. It took only a few hours of being oriented toward a career in business or accounting for me to eliminate these fields as a professional possibility; I felt totally uninspired.

Having already ruled out my first-choice career of professional baseball player because my skills didn't meet the job requirements, I found myself back at square one. It was late in the year, and thus my only option was to transfer to The City College of New York, Uptown, a liberal arts college in the middle of Harlem. The north campus of CCNY was architecturally beautiful, being one of the prime examples of Gothic architecture in the United States. There, I got a wonderful liberal arts education, majored in biology and was accepted into medical school.

College was a very exciting time for me. We were in the middle of the Vietnam War, great social upheaval was afoot, and expression of political freedoms was paramount. There were student sit-ins and riots at the college, and although I was only peripherally involved in them, a sense of social revolution permeated the entire culture. The rigid dogma of the past was being confronted by the explosiveness of personal freedom, and a clash of generations resulted. This created psychological turmoil, and I struggled with it for years afterward. The role models that I grew up with were suddenly rendered effete, and our absolute belief that The United States of America and its heroes were totally honorable was called into question. In the 1950s, the American public was scandalized after learning that Senator Joseph McCarthy had blacklisted anyone sympathetic to communism as an enemy of our country. When the motivations behind the Vietnam War came to light, many Americans began to question the righteousness of long-standing heroes. It also came to light that President Eisenhower was having an extramarital affair, and that General Douglas MacArthur's maniacal obsession with the Chinese communists had almost led us to the brink of nuclear war. The methods and ethics of many of our vaunted institutions, including J. Edgar Hoover's FBI, seemed murky at best. The whole military-industrial complex functioned as a self-serving entity, and people knew it. The entire meaning of patriotism came into question, and our nation found itself deeply divided.

One faction proclaimed: "America: Love or leave it!"

The other faction, who desired to challenge these social ills and to root out corruption, spoke loudly of their own kind of patriotism and love of country.

I consider the '60s to be the adolescence of American culture. It was a time in which the authority of cultural and moral values as well as political and religious institutions was called into sharp question, and things were never the same afterward.

See One! Do One! Teach One! Medical School Begins

The next stop was medical school, State University of New York Medical Center at Downstate, a.k.a. Downstate. My school's name invoked thoughts of a prison, which, in a way, it was. It was a place to which we were confined for most of each 24-hour day. There were numerous attempts to change the name, each of them more impersonal than the previous one.

The first day was overwhelming. Over 200 of the best and brightest students filled this cold, impressive space. I'd moved into a relatively new dormitory room several days before starting school, and my roommate, a somewhat arrogant chap, had come from Harvard University. Since I was only from the "Proletariat Harvard," the nickname given to CCNY during its most illustrious years, I was somewhat intimidated. Each room in the dormitory housed two students and had a bed and desk and shared a toilet with an adjacent neighbor. Our floors at that time were segregated by sex. We got to know each other up close and personal – warts and all – and I got to decide which of my dorm mates I felt comfortable with. These friendships would last through our school years and beyond.

I remember the orientation well. Most of it took place in an auditorium packed with more than 200 medical students as well as several graduate students. Initially, we were given a pep talk about the school and its success in developing capable physicians. We were also given an overview of the program, and then we got to meet the professors for our individual courses. Lectures were conducted in a large theater, where basic science lectures and demonstration films were presented.

Next we were brought to the labs. Up first was anatomy lab, and you knew where you were headed long before you'd entered the actual laboratory: the sweet, pungent aroma of formaldehyde, the preservative used to keep the cadavers fresh, wafted out into the hallway. Lab was conducted in an ordinary classroom containing 10 stainless steel tables, each covered with a tarpaulin, under which awaited a body ready for dissection. The class was divided into groups of four students, and each group worked with one body. Our professor was a petite woman barely older than we were: Dr. Sarah Weil, professor of anatomy. We were to spend four months together exploring the intricacies of the human body.

The next six weeks were overwhelming. The amount of information we were required to absorb was mind-boggling. Learning anatomy, which required learning the name of every muscle, bone, nerve and organ, was the equivalent of learning a new language, much of it derived from Latin or Greek. We spent all day in class. There were also several three- or four-hour labs each week, during which we dissected our cadavers. My group's cadaver was named "Larry," and we developed a personal relationship with him over time, even speculating about his profession and his lifestyle.

Prior to our dissection, we had to read our anatomy manuals, which were essentially road maps to the body with different chapters accentuating different organ systems. At the start, this meant tediously poring over pages and pages in which every word was novel and had to be defined by reviewing an even more extensive text. What was the relationship between this muscle and its insertion on that part of the bone? Or, which path did this nerve take to get from its origin in the brain to its ultimate destination of supplying sensation to three and a half fingers? This often necessitated evening trips back to the laboratory and studying until 2 or 3 in the morning. Unlike in college, it was then back to school the next day for another eight hours of classes. Despite the stress, I enjoyed the learning experience. Other subjects, especially biochemistry, sadly ended up on the back burner. After six weeks or so, the new words became familiar and I became more comfortable. However, my biochemistry grades were less than stellar, and I felt I needed to redirect my efforts.

During this time of refocusing, I seriously considered dropping out of medical school and joining the military. I ultimately decided against enlisting, a fortunate choice, as this was the most violent period of the Vietnam War. I saw myself as a plebeian from a lower-middle-class family whose parents had never graduated college, and also as a product of the public school system. This contrasted with the upbringings of many of my classmates. Their parents were professionals and they had attended private high school and acclaimed private colleges like MIT and the Ivy League schools. In addition, some of my classmates had unusual skills such as a photographic memory. These differences, coupled with my initial difficulty in budgeting my time among all of my subjects, engendered in me a great doubt about my capabilities. But I persevered, and I survived. Not everyone was so lucky. A suicide and a number of dropouts were among the victims claimed at Downstate. Some of my fellow students were not academically equipped for medical school, while others decided they were not well-suited for a career in medicine. There was also some question as to whether drugs and/or depression played a role in any of their decisions.

As I settled into the routine of medical school, I started making use of the brand new student center. To let out my pent-up anxiety, I took advantage of the yoga classes offered. Next, they started a basketball league in the new gym. I had never been much of a basketball player because I was somewhat uncoordinated. Some of that was due to my immaturity, as I was often two years younger than my classmates. In medical school, I expended all my extra energy on the basketball court until I developed knee pain. I didn't learn exactly what was causing the pain until I became a pediatrician myself: I had a common condition of athletic adolescents called Osgood-Schlatter disease, otherwise known as jumper's knee, which had resulted from my new athletic obsession. This condition resolves with maturity, so I guess I couldn't argue with one of my professors who mentioned in my evaluation that I was immature.

The first two years of medical school were didactic, which is to say, purely academic. In our immature estimations, the subjects we were studying did not have any direct relationship to our ultimate goal of becoming physicians. Little did we know, some of this arcane information was in fact closely related to disease processes and was laying vital groundwork for our later learning. There were lectures and labs for the basic sciences, anatomy and physiology and epidemiology, progressing to the individual organ systems: lungs, heart and kidneys. There were also lectures in pharmacology, taught by then-department chairman Dr. Robert Furchgott. He later won a Nobel Prize in medicine for clarifying the biochemical importance of nitric oxide in the human body. As it turns out, nitric oxide is essential to the development of penile erection in addition to less important bodily functions such as maintaining blood flow to the heart and brain. This discovery led to the subsequent discovery of the erectile dysfunction treatment drug Viagra and its competitors, whose advertisements depicting amorous older couples are ubiquitous in print, radio and television. It is ironic that this reserved professor's most lasting legacy will be penile tumescence and the image of a happy couple holding hands over the edges of side-by-side bathtubs.

During the first two years of medical school, we also took an epidemiology course. Epidemiology examines how disease spreads and can be controlled, but many of my classmates felt the material was irrelevant and refused to attend the class. Their protests took the form of a sit-down strike, which was a technique often invoked during The Tumultuous Sixties. I was among the participants who refused to attend the class.

Although we protesters consisted of at least a significant minority of the students in class, we were threatened by the administration and ultimately penalized when we weren't given credit for the course. There were no other repercussions. In retrospect, I still believe that the course as it was presented was irrelevant and in need of a major restructuring. Our action precipitated the revision of this extraneous course toward something more akin to public health.

Only toward the end of the second year did we move toward interacting directly with patients. We learned how to take a history and perform a physical exam by observing physician mentors and asking questions to patients with a specific disease. In this way, we learned in small groups the art and science of the physical examination. Because our medical school was affiliated with one of New York City's main public hospitals, patients who had the most advanced and unusual diseases were readily available. Our instructors were able to show us patients with dramatic findings to illustrate the value of certain diagnostic techniques: observation, auscultation, percussion and palpation (looking, listening, tapping out and feeling). Some patients had been so ravaged by tuberculosis that parts of their lungs were destroyed. This made it easy for us neophytes to distinguish between the healthy and unhealthy parts of the lungs using these techniques. We were able to fine-tune our neurological diagnostic skills by examining patients with the most dramatic findings. We also encountered patients who had experienced the devastation wrought on the nervous system by terminal syphilis. Clinical signs of syphilis included sensory changes and delusional thinking.

It was a very rare condition in that era, and treatment in the early stages was available.

In medical school, I learned that carefully listening to a patient's story and examining him or her properly will guide a physician to a correct diagnosis about 80 percent of the time. (These days, some of these skills have been forgotten or replaced by much less time-consuming but more costly hi-tech imaging techniques.)

The third and fourth years of medical school were filled with clinical courses in each area of medicine beginning with the basic medical specialties such as internal medicine, surgery, obstetrics, radiology, pediatrics and psychiatry. We would spend anywhere from four to 12 weeks in a field. In these courses, we would apply the basic sciences to the particular area of medicine by focusing on patient-specific problems. We arrived on the hospital wards at 7 a.m. and learned to do what was known as "scut work" – the routine or menial labor relegated to the junior intern. This included drawing blood, transporting patients to the radiology department and performing other kinds of testing. We organized the recent lab work, reported the patient's clinical progress by reviewing the charts, and then tried to present this information to the interns and residents actually responsible for the patient's medical care.

As we became more comfortable with handling our patients, we were given more and more opportunities to perform the different technical procedures necessary for the evaluation of the illnesses suffered by our wards. One of the principles of our education was: "See one, do one, teach one." Sometimes, though, it took more than just "one" try to get it right.

Eventually, we progressed to becoming the frontline in interviewing and examining the patients. I was very self-conscious about my uneasiness and my lack of familiarity with the process, and I felt much more comfortable examining an older, sicker patient than I did a younger patient. I identified more with these younger patients, and this might have made the prospect of caring for them more threatening. The chronic patients were much more tolerant of the prolonged time it took us to complete our task. Some of these patients actually craved the human contact.

As the old adage goes, though: "How do you get to Carnegie Hall? Practice! Practice! Practice!" Repetition of the process hundreds of times made me feel more comfortable with performing examinations. As I mastered the techniques, I warmed up to patient interactions, and I slowly transformed from a student into a physician.

At the end of our second year of medical school, we were introduced to the Clinical Pathological Conference (CPC), also known as morbidity-mortality Rounds (MMR).

These conferences aimed to instruct all physicians by presenting them with the case of an actual patient who had been evaluated and treated at the hospital. Discussing the case was supposed to help us to improve our diagnostic abilities and learn to come up with appropriate treatment plans. At these conferences, a resident or professor presented informative or very challenging cases. Extensive case histories, physical examinations, laboratory findings and radiology results were all recounted. Then, the audience was allowed to ask for further information.

One particular case we were presented with proved very challenging. The patient was a middle-aged man whose only symptoms were abdominal pain and weight loss. Little information could be gleaned from the physical examination and other supporting findings. The cause of the man's condition was only revealed when the autopsy was performed.

Before the professor revealed to us what had killed the man, he asked if anyone felt he or she could make the correct diagnosis.

A second-year medical student raised her hand and responded with great certainty: "Cancer of the head of the pancreas."

The professor then presented the pathological findings. Her deduction was correct. After the conference, the professor approached the student, amazed at her apparent clinical acumen.

"How did you come to your conclusion?" he asked.

She responded: "What else could it be?"

This line of thinking is not unusual for a doctor-in-training: medical students often look for clues that challenge their diagnostic abilities as they seek out the most esoteric and rare causes of particular clinical signs and symptom. As I'll discuss later, a physician should first consider the most common possible causes for a patient's problems. More experienced physicians always keep the rarer diseases in the backs of their heads, but they work to maintain proper perspective in order to make the correct diagnosis. As Sigmund Freud once observed, "Sometimes a cigar is just a cigar."

Other times, though, ignorance is bliss.

As we moved into our fourth year, we had the opportunity to choose elective courses in either the general fields we'd already studied or in even more subspecialized areas such as neurology (brain and nervous system), cardiology (heart), endocrinology (hormones), renal (kidney) or pulmonology (lung) medicine. This opportunity allowed us to think more seriously about the field of medicine we wanted to pursue. We were even allowed to take some of these electives at notable institutions outside of the purview of our school. I took advantage of this and spent three months in California.

Fine-Tuning the Instrument: Adding Experience to Knowledge

After my first year of medical school, I decided to treat myself to some time off. I took a $199 student flight to Amsterdam, with a stop in Iceland. From there, I meandered through Europe with no specific agenda on a budget of $5 a day. I slept in hostels or found room rentals posted at the train stations. I took trains, rode to Barcelona on the back of a motorcycle and saw a bullfight, visited relatives and looked for cheap student flights to determine my next destination. This lifestyle was quite a contrast from the structure of medical school. I would wake up each day and decide where I wanted to go, if anywhere. I visited most of the sites and museums from Amsterdam to Rome, from Nice to London. I visited more than 10 countries during that summer. I loved wandering down the streets, speaking to the locals and exploring the food and culture, and my most memorable experiences involved other people.

I fell in love twice, both times without reciprocation. The first time was in England with a young lady I named "Maid Marion."

She had chestnut hair, soft brown eyes and a great British accent. She did not share my amorous intentions.

The next fantasy romance involved a Danish girl, Jeanette, who had golden hair and saucer-sized, almond-shaped green eyes. We met in Italy when I extricated her from an uncomfortable situation with several Romans. She and a friend were being harassed by some persistent local males at an outdoor cafe. I came over to her and indicated to these "gentlemen" that she was with me. Honorably, they left. She gave me her phone number, which inspired me to fly to Copenhagen.

There, I met her parents, went with her to some nightclubs and saw some of the local sights, including The Little Mermaid and Hamlet's Castle. They were just so hospitable. Unfortunately, she had a boyfriend. We parted as friends and communicated by letter for a short time.

On another occasion I was strolling through the British Museum and came across an old man in crumpled clothes painting a copy of an Anthony Van Dyck masterpiece, "Portrait of Cornelius van der Geest, c. 1620." I thought he was a struggling artist. I was struck by the painting and I asked him if I could buy his rendition, as it reminded me of my goateed grandfather. The man said it was not for sale, as it was unfinished, but he gave me his address and invited me to his studio.

Later that week I took a train from London to the suburb of Rickmansworth. I was expecting to find a modest structure, and I was surprised to encounter instead a modern wooden and glass frame home with an entirely open vista facing the woods. It was not grand, but it was strikingly beautiful. He served me tea and we conversed for well over an hour. He turned out to be the famous artist Arthur Pan, who had painted the Winston Churchill portrait that hung in the White House during Franklin Roosevelt's administration. He insisted I buy one of his paintings. Not insulted by my meek budget, he selected a painting for me. I am sure it was not one of his finest, but it was a very lovely floral piece that I hauled in its frame all the way back to the United States. It hangs in my home to this day.

My next two summers were not as adventurous, but they were full of new experiences all the same. I spent the following summer at Mount Sinai Hospital in New York doing a sub-internship in neurology under the tutelage of Morris Bender, MD, a singular physician who could often determine the exact location of a brain abnormality simply by taking an extensive history and doing a careful physical exam. Today, we use CAT scans and MRIs. He was so single-minded that when he listened to the music of Wolfgang Amadeus Mozart what he visualized was nystagmus, an abnormal eye movement present in a number of neurological conditions. I guess you could say he had a one-track mind.

During that summer I was again reminded of the importance of doing a thorough patient history and physical examination when determining a diagnosis. CAT scans and MRIs didn't yet exist. The further testing available to us at the time was invasive and included procedures such as the cerebral angiogram, in which a radiographic dye was injected through an artery to help a doctor visualize the brain. In another radiographic procedure called the pneumoencephalogram, contrast material was injected into the spinal canal to enable the physician to view the fluid spaces around the spinal cord and brain.

I remember the case of a teenage girl suffering from severe, crippling headaches who suddenly died after a spinal tap was performed on her for diagnostic purposes. The autopsy was inconclusive, but it was presumed she had increased pressure in her brain, which caused the brain to herniate in response to the tap. This compressed the brainstem, which controls heart rate and breathing. These days, such tragedies can sometimes be avoided by performing noninvasive headache tests for diagnostic purposes.

Another teenage patient I encountered developed sudden agitation, then became delirious, then comatose, then died. The autopsy revealed an unusual neurological complication of measles. I also came across unusual movement disorders, brain tumors, multiple sclerosis, seizure disorders and strokes, amongst other diseases. I found that using all the clinical diagnostic tools at my disposal to make the correct diagnosis was very exciting. It was like solving a mystery. Unfortunately, at that time there was little treatment available for most of those conditions. As interesting as these intellectual exercises were, I could not see myself ever enjoying being able to tell a patient what the problem was unless I could also offer treatment options.

I spent the next summer in a research department with the world's authority on a specific endocrinological disease called adrenogenital syndrome (also known as congenital adrenal hyperplasia, or CAH). In this illness, a block in one or more steps of a biochemical pathway affects the production of cortisone and sex hormones. These deficiencies are potentially fatal and can result in ambiguous sexual organs in infants. Thus, genetic girls could have the external sexual structures of boys and vice versa. It was subsequently determined that milder abnormalities could cause more subtle changes in women later on in life.

It was a unique experience that enabled me to see directly the effect such arcane biochemical processes could have on a person. Early in my career, I had a newborn patient named "John" who did well for the first six or seven days of life. He then began to vomit. Physically, he appeared fine, so we checked into common conditions such as formula intolerance. When he started losing weight and becoming less energetic, we had him admitted to the hospital, where he was diagnosed with CAH. Muddled external sex organs are usually the most obvious indicator of the syndrome, but the block in the steps of cortisone formation hadn't affected John's external genitalia, so it was a tricky diagnosis to make.

John has been on replacement cortisone therapy since that time, and his dose is adjusted based on stress or illness to avoid sending him into shock. Treatment has created its own problems for John, such as osteoporosis, which resulted in a fracture of his spine and foot. John eventually grew up and went to college, but his education was interrupted by another illness: inflammatory bowel disease. It sidelined him for several years. John ultimately became an emergency medical technician. He was then accepted to a new medical school in Tennessee and he has just graduated and started his residency. John is also engaged to be married. When I recently called to congratulate him, I joked to him that he was the only medical student who never had to open a text, as he'd personally experienced every disease in the book.

At the time, we also tested for growth hormone deficiency with a stimulation test. This test was performed in children with growth problems and low growth hormone levels. In those cases, two medications were administered intravenously to determine if the brain was capable of producing adequate levels of this hormone that is so necessary to proper growth. This evaluation was in its infancy at that time. It was risky and had to be closely monitored, as the patient could develop low blood sugar and potentially go into shock.

Spending my residency in that medical ward was like being in a museum filled with examples of the most rare medical conditions that can affect the human body. We also saw unusual metabolic disorders in which the body was not able to break down basic body chemicals, which resulted in the abnormal toxic accumulation of these products. The consequence was often deformity and death. We were a center for two of these diseases: Hurler disease and Hunter disease. (These two are now classified as syndromes.)

Less commonly, we saw more ordinary endocrine diseases. The usual ratio of common to uncommon endocrinological conditions was 10: or 20:1, but that ratio was reversed in this medical unit. It was an exciting day for the residents when a child being evaluated for weight loss, rapid heartbeat and heat intolerance turned out to simply have hyperthyroidism (excess thyroid hormone), or when another patient with weight loss, excessive drinking and urination turned out to have diabetes rather than an unusual brain tumor.

A Fork in the Road: Choosing Pediatrics

At the time when I was struggling to choose an area of postgraduate training, a cynical adage was floating around about the various specialties: "The internist knows everything but does nothing. The surgeon knows nothing but does everything. The psychiatrist knows nothing and does nothing. The pathologist knows everything but knows it too late."

Many of my fellow medical students had an idea of the area of medicine they wanted to pursue early on. Others had a preconception and the remainder had no idea. The undecided among us had open minds and would choose after rotating through the various specialties. I think the students who had the greatest exposure to the practice of medicine prior to medical school, either through having a physician parent or working in a medical setting, were most likely to decide earlier on in their schooling. The best decisions were made based on the medical student's skill sets, level of manual dexterity, intellectual proclivities and personality. And certain personality types seemed to have a tendency to go into certain specialties: surgeons were somewhat brash with big egos that tended to enlarge with the increasing degree of specialization.

The neurosurgeons and cardiac surgeons were closest to God. The most cerebral were the internists, including those in subspecialties such as neurology, endocrinology and nephrology and pathology. The most empathic were the psychiatrists. Radiologists and anesthesiologists tended to be less social, which was not a problem in those fields due to the limited patient interaction required. Pediatricians were usually kind, gregarious and somewhat childlike. Because of those qualities, we connect best to children.

In my class you could count on one hand the number of people who chose a specialty based on earning potential. This seems to have changed somewhat recently with the increasing debt that medical students now incur and the reimbursement policies of government and insurance companies. Medical students can now emerge from school with the equivalent of a half-million-dollar mortgage, with anywhere from three to seven years of additional training ahead. I hope this will change as we are trending toward a severe shortage of primary care physicians. (Having taught medical students for the past 15 years, I can say with reasonable certainty that the current group of medical students is intelligent and dedicated.)

My personal decision was based partially on my understanding of my own personal strengths and weaknesses. A lack of manual dexterity eliminated the surgical specialties. I enjoy interacting with patients, which excluded radiology and anesthesiology. Although I realized many of my patients' symptoms originated in the mind, I didn't feel comfortable in the skin of a psychiatrist. I was torn between pediatrics and internal medicine.

During my last year of medical school I took two rotations in very fine programs in California. The first program was nephrology at a UCLA affiliate at Harbor General Hospital with one of the premier kidney specialists at the time, Richard Glassock, MD. The other elective was a general pediatric sub-internship at Los Angeles Children's Hospital. Going through these programs helped me to realize that although I enjoy taking care of sick patients, I need to be able to make them well. Children can get very sick extremely quickly, but they can usually be cured with proper treatment. Treating older patients involves dealing with chronic illness, which means "cure" is not in the vocabulary. Geriatricians care specifically for the aged, a calling also not suited to my temperament. (Fortunately we have physicians with all of these varied qualities, as we need doctors to populate all of these fields.)

After four long years of arduous training, most of which I found challenging yet enjoyable, I graduated. For those of my fellow male medical students who were married while in school, the demands often meant the kiss of death. Medical school was hard on wives, as in essence, the medical student and subsequent young doctor had two wives: the first wife was medicine, and the second was his wife by marriage.

At graduation time, we recited the *Oath of Maimonides*, named after the brilliant physician and philosopher of the Middle Ages who originally penned the words:

> The eternal providence has appointed me to watch over the life and health of Thy creatures. May the love for my art actuate me at all time; may neither avarice nor miserliness, nor thirst for glory or for a great reputation engage my mind; for the enemies of truth and philanthropy could easily deceive me and make me forgetful of my lofty aim of doing good to Thy children.
>
> May I never see in the patient anything but a fellow creature in pain.
>
> Grant me the strength, time and opportunity always to correct what I have acquired, always to extend its domain; for knowledge is immense and the spirit of man can extend indef-

initely to enrich itself daily with new requirements. Today he can discover his errors of yesterday and tomorrow he can obtain a new light on what he thinks himself sure of today.

Oh, God, Thou has appointed me to watch over the life and death of Thy creatures; here am I ready for my vocation and now I turn unto my calling.

TWO

Residency and Beyond

I WAS 24 YEARS OLD when I graduated medical school. I'd been in school for 20 years at that point, and I'd only recently completed puberty. I was not ready to assume the responsibility of the life-and-death decisions that physicians must make. I needed a timeout, referred to these days as a "gap year." If I'd been born in another country, I would have entered into a compulsory two-year military stint. But I was a product of the American '60s, and I needed to explore the essence of my being instead.

I decided to take a year off to determine if my motives were pure for going into this esteemed profession, or if I'd just been on autopilot. By the year's end, I arduously came to the conclusion that pediatrics was, indeed, my calling.

A Prelude to Doctoring: Adventures in Residency

During my year off, I again had to choose a residency. I did not attend the program I'd been matched to during medical school, which was Mount Sinai Hospital in New York. Instead, I attended Lenox Hill Hospital, which was known as a "Sleeper Program." It was lower key than the big academic programs, but it was affiliated with a number of the big centers. Most of the necessary specialists were available, and we were able to consult with others from the affiliated medical centers. Interns and residents were able to manage all service patients and even many of the private patients if we earned the trust of the attending physicians. We were able to order tests, perform procedures, prescribe treatment plans and call in the appropriate consults. We also had a New York City emergency room, which brought ambulance cases to the hospital.

We started call on the first day of July – the traditional start of internships and residencies. There, we were introduced to our senior residents and learned of our job responsibilities. We were to be on call every third night and every third weekend. At the time, this meant starting the day at 7 a.m. and remaining in the hospital caring for patients, attending lectures and rounds and researching patients' conditions until 5 p.m. the next day. During rounds, you'd present your patients' conditions, medications and the result of all the recent testing to the senior residents and attending physicians. Afterward, a discussion would ensue, during which a care plan including treatment and further testing was created. After signing out, usually between 5 and 6 p.m., the on-call intern was responsible for all the pediatric patients on the hospital ward, with the backup of senior residents and ultimately the attending pediatrician. In our case, we also had to cover the emergency room and the delivery room.

Being asked to devote myself to the patients for these prolonged periods of time allowed me to follow the course of an illness and to see responses to treatment in real time. This intensive patient involvement also allowed me to develop a concentrated relationship with the patient and his or her disease, which proved invaluable in the care of future patients. This residency setup ended in the 1980s with the untimely death of Libby Zion. Libby was an 18-year-old college freshman whose father happened to be a *New York Times* reporter. She was seen at New York Hospital because of flu-like symptoms. She'd been taking an antidepressant (which had been discontinued) and possibly other medications. There was no diagnosis at the time of admission, and Libby became increasingly agitated. She was treated for her agitation and had a sudden cardiac arrest.

She was being managed by an intern and resident in consultation with her private doctor. After Libby died, it was determined that the medications used to treat her agitation had interacted with other medications she was taking, which resulted in her death. Whether or not this situation occurred because of the physician's inexperience with this medical condition was unimportant to Libby's father. Young physicians' long hours became his scapegoat, and he lobbied hard to limit the hours of medical interns and residents. He eventually won, and the Libby Zion Law was passed, which limited the workweek for interns and residents to 80 hours and not more than 24 hours in succession.

The patient population at Lenox Hill was varied, from the wealthy Park and Fifth avenues crowd to the indigent. Of the poorer patients, the most unique were the Gypsies, who are now referred to as the Roma and Sinti. They all seemed to list their addresses as the best in New York: Park and Fifth avenues or Central Park West. When the hospital had one of their children as a patient, the gypsies would swarm into the hospital by as many as 30 at a time. The men, women and children would camp out and we'd be inundated by questions from various adult members of the tribe. HIPAA (Health Insurance Portability and Accountability Act) privacy rules didn't yet exist, and they all insisted they were mothers, fathers, aunts and uncles.

At that time, I read an exposé in *New York Magazine* about Gypsy culture in New York City. According to the article, each clan had its own chief or king, and the next time I was approached by a band of questioners, I asked to be introduced to the king, insisting that I would only speak to him and that he alone would transmit the information to rest of the clan. I earned the trust of these leaders, and life at the hospital got easier.

Some cases remain fresh in a physician's mind for years, popping up whenever a similar case presents itself, and a few from this period of my early career still stand out for me. I'll never forget "Frankie," an Eastern European adolescent who came to the hospital the day before Thanksgiving after he fell down while ice skating. He'd hit the back of his head and he'd momentarily lost consciousness. Frankie was evaluated in the emergency room and released after he was thoroughly evaluated and his skull x-ray came back normal. (CAT scans weren't available at the time.)

On Thanksgiving Day, he was brought back to the emergency room in an agitated and confused state. Soon, he "blew a pupil," a situation in which the pupil of the eye dilates and becomes unresponsive to light. The pupil is the opening that lets light into the retina (the visual processing area), and a blown pupil indicates severe pressure in the brain. He then lost consciousness. Frankie was immediately brought up to the operating room, where the neurosurgeon opened Frankie's skull and removed the blood that had been causing the pressure. Medical treatments to relieve pressure were prescribed, but the damage was already done and Frankie remained unresponsive. He was eventually transferred to a long-term care facility.

"Rachel" was an 8-year-old girl under the care of a reputable private pediatrician. He had seen her numerous times over the prior week for the diagnosis of flu. It was winter: flu season. Her doctor finally sent her to the hospital when she developed abdominal pain and vomiting. He was concerned about an intestinal obstruction. What probably started as flu had by then morphed into a severe pneumonia, with pus in the lung cavity. (The pneumonia was the cause of the intestinal symptoms.) Shortly after being admitted to the hospital, Rachel went into shock and kidney failure and never recovered. This case is in the back of my mind every time I see a child with prolonged fever and flu-like symptoms.

"Stacey's" case was also sad and disturbing, but it's a good illustration of the unusual twists and turns that can complicate even fairly common diseases, and of the toll illness can take on a family. Stacey was an 11-year-old African-American female who had been sent to the hospital by her private physician for vaginal bleeding. In fact, it was rectal bleeding. She went on to develop the most severe case of Crohn's disease I've ever seen. The disease eventually resulted in the emergency surgical removal of her large bowel. Subsequently she developed an overwhelming bacterial infection. She even lost the ability to do mathematical calculations, presumably due to a stroke, which can be a rare complication of Crohn's disease. By the time she was discharged, Stacey was debilitated and neurologically impaired and the structure of her intact family was destroyed. Her parents subsequently divorced.

"Ali" was a 6-year-old boy visiting from Bangladesh who was admitted to our hospital for an evaluation of bruising. After we'd determined that he did not have leukemia, we were able to make the diagnosis of idiopathic thrombocytopenic purpura (ITP). It's quite a mouthful, but translated into plain English, this means that Ali had a low blood platelet count without a known cause. In fact, the body produces antibodies against platelets, which are an important factor in blood clotting. Thus, a deficiency can result in bruising and other bleeding-related consequences. He was treated and his platelet count improved, but it didn't reach a normal level. This persisted for six months with no new bruising.

As the time for Ali to return to Bangladesh approached, we had to make a decision about the course of his treatment. There was intense debate about whether we should remove the spleen, which would permanently resolve the low platelet issue, or just leave him alone. His current platelet count was safe but if it dropped in response to a viral infection he could have more bleeding issues. Since he was returning to a developing country, we were also concerned that removing the spleen would reduce his immunity and make him more prone to infections, especially those caused by parasites. We decided to observe Ali. He returned 12 months later and his platelet count and condition were stable.

An inspirational early case was that of Maria de los Milagros. Maria was the product of two older immigrant parents who had been trying to conceive for years. Finally a baby was born, 16 weeks early, and she was named accordingly: in English, her name meant "Mary of the Miracles." Maria flew through the neonatal intensive care unit with barely a hiccup as the other premature babies struggled with breathing and repeated infections and even sometimes died. Even today, with our sophisticated newborn care technologies, it is still unusual for a baby as premature as Maria to do so well after birth.

In the spring of my internship, during my first year of training, I rotated through Memorial Hospital for Cancer and Allied Diseases, with one month on the inpatient service and one month in the clinic. The early '70s marked the dawn of successful cancer treatment, and different chemotherapeutic and radiation therapies were being formulated and used to treat people. Today, many cancers are treatable and even curable, thanks to these early milestones. Prior to the 1970s, though, the diagnosis of cancer was a death sentence. When I was 11, a strapping and previously healthy teenage neighbor of mine was diagnosed with Hodgkin's disease. The only treatment available at the time was cortisone, which brought just temporary relief. He was dead in six months.

By the time I began my rotation, the medical field was seeing some real success in the treatment of leukemia and Hodgkin's disease. The rest was trial and error. The most difficult cases wound up at Memorial Sloan Kettering Hospital, often as a last hope.

Black humor is often the only technique a medical professional can use to survive witnessing the ravages of suffering at such an intense level. Many healthcare providers use this defense as a coping mechanism. Mark, an intern with a dry sense of humor, preceded me at Memorial. Mark began his initial rounds on the ward by being introduced to his first patient, a 7- or 8-year-old boy whose head was deformed by numerous cancerous growths. After presenting the case, the attending physician asked Mark if he had any questions. As a way of dealing with his anxiety, Mark replied: "Just tell me! Is this my worst patient?"

Many other treatments also remained relatively primitive. The correct medications, doses and treatment combinations had yet to be perfected. Patients experienced all kinds of complications, and they would often be in the hospital for months. As a neophyte physician, this situation presented me with a very exciting challenge. I would diagnose and treat conditions that were so rare they were only read about in textbooks. Unfortunately, the excitement wore off as I personally experienced the toll of the treatments and disease on these unfortunate children and their families. After witnessing the last gasping breath of "Scotty," a boy dying from neuroblastoma, I lost my appetite for this subspecialty, and as I developed into a mature physician, the relief and joy of informing patients that they were medically well far outweighed the excitement of diagnosing an unusual disease.

Another important thing I learned during this time was how essential it is to respect – and to earn the return respect of – the nursing staff. This was an important tool crucial to surviving my early years in the hospital. If nurses felt that a doctor was earnest, hardworking and appreciative of their role in the process of caring for patients, they worked to make that doctor's life much easier. If, on the other hand, a doctor displayed a superior attitude or was dismissive of their input, they could make that doctor's life rather hellish. No good nurse would ever do anything to compromise a patient's well-being, of course, but that didn't mean a nurse couldn't make a doctor's life miserable in a million small ways. If a disliked doctor was on the night shift, for example, a nurse might call him or her repeatedly throughout the course of the night with requests for a multitude of non-urgent tasks (such as blood tests) that could easily have been performed at the same time.

My natural inclination is to respect and be courteous toward all people unless they prove undeserving, and I saw nurses as an invaluable set of additional eyes and ears, as they spent much more time with each individual patient than I did. In return, they gifted me with the rare pleasure of six straight hours of sleep one night while I was covering the neonatal intensive care unit.

A positive offshoot of my experience at Memorial Hospital was my encounter with one particular nurse, Kathleen. She was adorable, and she was to become my future wife. She was cute and prissy, dressed meticulously in a starched white uniform and perfectly clean white shoes. Kathleen was extremely caring, smart, diligent and energetic in a way that calls to mind, in retrospect, Mother Teresa. Ironically, Kathy's impression of me in my white, starched intern's attire, with my beard, full head of hair (at the time) and piercing blue eyes, was that I was something of a Jesus-like figure. She later told me if she'd happened to meet me when I was dressed in my usual manner, that sacred image would've been severely tarnished. We began dating. Within six weeks, we were engaged. Within six months, we were married, and we are still together to this day.

The people we encounter often shape our lives, and our admiration or disdain for them can affect the way we behave far into the future. Sam Stone, MD, an old-time pediatrician at New York University, was someone who guided my life and whom I tried to emulate. He was always available for a call if you had a problem with a patient and he would often come into the hospital after hours to help out with a difficult patient in the intensive care unit, even if the patient wasn't his own. He was soft-spoken and never demeaning. When I was planning for my third-year residency electives, I called Dr. Stone for advice. I asked him whether I should take an elective in nephrology (the study of kidneys) or in cardiology. He laughed and asked me how many cases from either of these specialties I actually expected to encounter each year in private practice as a pediatrician. He suggested that I take an elective in learning disabilities instead, and I did. It was probably the most useful program for private practice that I ever could have taken.

Dr. Stefania Kennessey was my intern during my first year of residency. Although I supervised Stefanie, she'd been a board-certified pediatrician in Hungary for more than a decade. Her husband, Zoltan, had gotten a job with the United Nations and they'd moved to New York. She raised two children and decided to return to pediatrics. She had to pass a proficiency exam for foreign-trained doctors and then she had to repeat her entire pediatric training. We made a great team. I taught her current protocols and technological advances, and she provided me with the benefit of her years of pediatric experience. We became close friends. My wife and I even attended her daughter's wedding. Later, she and Zoltan defected from Hungary and were forced to move to Washington, DC, where he worked at the Federal Reserve. We've been in touch ever since.

And then there was "Dr. Arnie", a man often referred to as "Uncle Arnie" by his patients. Dr. Arnie was a celebrity doctor who had many famous patients. He was charming and witty and I personally liked the guy, but in my humble opinion, he was a lousy pediatrician. He'd often portray his patient's illnesses as being more serious than they really were, and he admitted many children unnecessarily. When these youngsters recovered, Dr. Arnie became their savior, but his approach also resulted in a slew of overanxious parents. One weekend when I was on call, I found myself inundated with the admission of sick children, including a few of Dr. Arnie's less severe patients. I called him up and jokingly warned him that if he admitted another of his bogus cases I would be less than happy. He honored my wishes. Monday morning, he proudly walked over to me to get my personal thanks for his kind consideration. Dr. Arnie was definitely a role model whose approach I worked hard *not* to imitate.

Patients Are People, Too: What They Do and Don't Teach You in Residency

What did I learn in residency? I learned to assess and to manage the most serious medical problems. I could handle anything from an acute seizure disorder to diabetes, asthma to dehydration, anemia and even acute leukemia as well as newborn emergencies and most nonsurgical problems. We had a clinic several times a week in which we were the primary caregivers for local children without doctors. There, we learned to treat the basic illnesses that pediatricians see in their offices: sore throats, ear infections, coughs, colds, rashes, vomiting and diarrhea.

We also learned that doctors glean a lot more information by listening than they do by talking. A thorough doctor is not necessarily a doctor who orders a lot of tests but one who listens carefully, asks the right questions and performs a good examination, letting the patient talk and keeping in mind, always, that old adage: First, do no harm. (Unfortunately, some therapies do have side effects, in which case, the treatment should never be worse than the problem.)

Edward Davies, MD, the head of the department of pediatrics during my residency at Lenox Hill Hospital, imparted some additional helpfully straightforward wisdom: The longer you've been sick, the longer it takes to get better. It's an intuitive concept, but it seems to get lost on many of my patients. I recently examined a college student who had been coughing for two weeks. I asked him if the cough was better, worse or the same. He said that it was unchanged.

My next question: "What brought you in today?"

The patient then told me he was leaving for Argentina with his parents that night. It turned out he had a clinical pneumonia, although he wasn't very sick. Had he been sicker, there is no way I would've gotten him better in time. I've seen this story played out in my office hundreds of times with countless patients and events. Many salvageable trips have been canceled after an illness was left to linger too long.

What we *didn't* learn in residency was how to deal with chronic behavioral or psychological issues, and we emerged ill-prepared to deal with the complex interactions between parents and their children that can contribute to disease. Solving such problems is an important part of what a pediatrician does, and when we address them, disease and illness can be significantly reduced.

The value of a good history and a good patient-physician relationship cannot be overstated when it comes to dealing with these kinds of problems. Awhile back, I saw a 2-year-old girl, "Jennifer," who suffered from recurring fevers. The girl was brought to me by her father and her grandmother, with whom I'd worked with at our local hospital. The patient's parents were not married and they shared joint custody of the girl. The mother had repeatedly brought the child to the physician and to the hospital emergency rooms for high fevers. But when the father had the child, everything seemed fine.

The grandmother was concerned about Munchausen by proxy syndrome, a condition that occurs when a caregiver concocts an illness, in this case, in a child, for some kind of psychological gain. If this goes unchecked, the child can develop into an adult preoccupied by illness who visits doctors and hospitals repeatedly. This is not only expensive but also disruptive to the person's life.

In the case of this 2-year-old girl, the visits caused significant friction and anger to develop between the parents. I intervened by first evaluating Jennifer and communicating to both parents that my only concern was their daughter's health. I tried to establish the importance of consistent care with one pediatrician. The mom lived several hours away so that was not entirely possible, but I encouraged her to go to one pediatrician instead of to multiple healthcare facilities, and to keep records of each illness. I continued to get calls from the father about these often-monthly visits to the other physician for fevers and sore throats, which were treated with antibiotics. This is an unusual situation for a 2-year-old, so I spoke with the other pediatrician. During this period I received a frantic call from the father, who was worried about another unnecessary visit to a hospital that had resulted in radiation exposure due to a CAT scan of the head. This situation arose when Jennifer supposedly fell back and hit her head. The child had no bump or bruise. This again aroused the father's suspicion of unnecessary medical visits.

At the time of her fall, the girl had been staying with her maternal grandmother, who, according to the father, was herself preoccupied with illness. I decided to call the mom directly to take a careful history of the event. What I learned was that the child had been crying, held her breath, and passed out momentarily, at which point she fell and hit her head. Grandma was appropriately concerned and called 9-1-1. When the child arrived at the hospital, she was fine and had no bruises, but an x-ray was taken for precautionary purposes.

I told both mom and dad that it was a reasonable decision for grandma to call 9-1-1. Mom felt reassured that I was not trying to incriminate her. Jennifer was now brought to me for her illnesses, and I noted a pattern to those illnesses, with periodic fevers and tonsillitis. I made a tentative diagnosis of PFAPA (periodic fever, aphthous stomatitis, pharyngitis and adenitis), a somewhat unusual situation in which a child can develop fevers, mouth sores, tonsillitis and even swollen glands, usually every three to four weeks. No antibiotics are needed. Most commonly, there is no specific identifiable cause. I ordered some blood tests to reassure myself that there was not a more serious underlying illness. The girl was then referred to a specialist who confirmed the diagnosis and recommended a treatment course. Mom and dad were now reassured that their daughter did not have a serious disease and they were given the tools to manage the child's fevers without repeated visits to physicians and to hospital emergency rooms. She was no longer a "frequent flyer" in our medical care system.

More rewarding for me than making the diagnosis was seeing mom and dad together at their daughter's 3-Year Checkup acting very civilly toward each other with their attention focused appropriately on Jennifer rather than on the mutual anger that had built up between them. Avoiding finger-pointing, unmasking the cause of the child's repeated illnesses and winning the trust of both parents that my main concern was their daughter's health allowed me to encourage this cordial relationship, which created a much healthier environment for my patient.

Some important skills in a pediatrician's repertoire cannot be taught to medical students, but must be gleaned by experience, either with patients or with one's own children. Even the day-to-day issues that parents face with their children were only superficially addressed during residency. For example: How much food do you offer a baby? How do you handle a baby who fights going to sleep? What do you do to minimize an older child's reaction to a new baby in the house? To help me answer these and many other questions that my early patient interactions brought to the fore, I bought Dr. Benjamin Spock's iconic work, *Baby and Child Care*, and I read it from cover to cover before starting private practice. It proved a valuable resource.

Flying Solo: The Pediatrician Emerges

In June 1976, I started private practice at Chestnut Ridge Pediatrics in Woodcliff Lake, New Jersey. I had hoped to remain in Manhattan, but there were a limited number of babies being born there and private practitioners were not embracing new competitors. I had interviewed at several practices around New York City and New Jersey, and I certainly did not expect to cross the Hudson River and move out west to set up shop.

I can still recall a 1976 *The New Yorker* magazine cover that pictured a map of Manhattan, the Hudson River, New Jersey, "No Man's Land" and the Pacific Ocean. I was a native New Yorker who felt like Davy Crockett moving to the wild frontier, even though the area in which I was settling was barely west of the Hudson River and within 25 minutes' drive of New York City.

Chestnut Ridge Pediatrics was founded close to 60 years ago by Robert Sapin, MD, whom I replaced upon his retirement. I was very fortunate to join a practice whose partners were good physicians and honest, fair people: Donald Wolmer, MD, and Alan Benstock, MD. We worked together for more than 30 years, at which point Don and then Alan retired. They still come around periodically to pester us at the office. Since CRPA's founding, only one physician has left the practice in a manner other than retirement. (That physician, Joseph Kramer, MD, left to set up a practice in an indigent area of New York City. He then became an icon and was even featured on a segment of the TV show *60 Minutes*.)

During my first three weeks at Chestnut Ridge, I oriented myself to the patients and to the office setup. I did not yet have call, meaning

I had no solo responsibility and I always had an associate around for support and reassurance. Afterward, my life as a pediatrician really began. I was on call every third night and every third weekend for 14 years, until our next associate, Mark Mandel, MD, joined us. One of the big differences from residency at that time was the lack of backup. When you were on call, you were it, and there were no senior residents or attending physicians to turn to for advice. The buck stopped with me, and my first week on call was a doozy. I had to call on all of my recent experience as a resident just to survive.

My first charge was "Luke," a 12-month-old twin boy who had Down's syndrome and heart disease. He was brought to the office because he was having difficulty breathing. I determined that he had heart failure and decided to admit him to the hospital. I ran down to the hospital just in time for Luke's first cardiac arrest. I resuscitated him and arranged a transport to a pediatric intensive care unit. His heart stopped two more times before the ICU transport arrived. Unfortunately, he succumbed to his illness within the next several days.

My next challenge was "Christopher," who was 11. His mom called on a Sunday night, concerned about his sore throat. It didn't seem to be an emergency, so I told her to give Chris some Tylenol, have him gargle and encourage fluids. Mom called again shortly after and I didn't have much to add, although I did tell her to call me back if there was any vomiting or difficulty breathing. Half an hour later, I received a call letting me know that Chris had started vomiting. Back then, there were no emergency room pediatricians so I again rushed down and met them in the ER. When I saw him I immediately knew what the problem was. He was not vomiting because of an intestinal infection but because he could not swallow his saliva. He was seated with his neck and chest extended forward, agitated and in extreme distress. Chris was suffering from epiglottitis, an extreme medical emergency. (Fortunately, we don't see this disease any more, as there is a vaccine given to infants and children to prevent it.) He could stop breathing at any time.

Chris was in need of an emergency airway, which in those days meant a tracheostomy. (During a tracheostomy, a tube is surgically implanted into the windpipe, below the voice box or Adam's apple, in the neck.) We called an otolaryngologist immediately and kept Chris upright, as lying him down would further compromise his airway. He was then brought to the operating room, where a tracheostomy was successfully performed, bypassing the problem. Next, we gave him antibiotics, as his condition had been caused by the bacteria *Haemophilus influenza* Group B. Within two to three days, he had no fever, his epiglottis had normalized and the tracheostomy tube was removed. Chris grew into a strapping young man, and the only remnant of our encounter was a small scar on his neck.

"Guy" was a 3-and-a-half-year-old asthmatic who tormented my associates and me for years. He was one of the two worst asthmatics I encountered over the course of my entire career. In the early 1980s, the treatment for an acute asthmatic attack was more primitive and hands-on than it is today. We would meet the patient in the office or emergency room, assess him to assure ourselves that there were no other medical problems, and start treatment with adrenaline injections. After the first shot, we'd reevaluate in 20 to 30 minutes, and if the patient wasn't completely better, we'd give another shot, repeating this up to three times before we declared "status asthmaticus." Inhaled medications didn't exist at that time. If the patient was still uncomfortable, we'd then advise admission. At that point, we'd begin intravenous fluids and steroids along with medications rarely given today due to their potential side effects. Medication dosages had to be carefully calculated.

Guy was considered a frequent flyer, and he was being optimally treated on a daily basis, with frequent monitoring of dosages in consultation with a specialist. Despite this and despite the diligent care of his mom, whenever he got a cold, we'd need to meet him, and he was admitted many times each year. Guy was one of only two asthmatics I cared for who required intubation and the use of a respirator to survive an attack, and he taught me a very important lesson. Fresh out of training, I believed that if a treatment failed to work for a patient, it was because the physician had failed at his job. This belief still persists in the medical field, but the truth is that sometimes you can do everything right and the outcome is still unsatisfactory. So much for the godlike powers of physicians! After more than 10 years of repeated hospitalizations, several intubations and even two pneumothoraces (a condition where the lungs can blow out like balloons because of the extreme pressures needed to sustain adequate air exchange), Guy finally grew out of his asthma.

I encountered "Peter," a 3-week-old baby, on a Sunday. He had been doing fine earlier in the day, but as is often the case, his mother became more concerned about his illness as nighttime approached. She called me for reassurance and advice on the appropriate medicine to treat a fever with few accompanying symptoms. Because of his young age, I was concerned about a serious, life-threatening illness and had them meet me immediately in the emergency room. There, I encountered a baby in the early stages of shock. I performed a sepsis workup, which included blood work, a chest x-ray and a spinal tap. He had a serious bacterial meningitis, which can be passed to a baby as he travels through the mother's birth canal, but usually doesn't manifest until three to four weeks after birth. He was immediately started on intravenous antibiotics. Peter made a complete recovery without any complications. I continued to see him into his adolescence, and he excelled in school. This type of bacterial meningitis is rarely seen these days, as women are monitored during their pregnancy for the asymptomatic bacteria and treated prior to delivery if it is present.

THREE

An Approach to Care

OVER THE DECADES following my baptism by fire into full-time pediatric practice, I've continued to hone my approach to care. I've learned over time that being a good physician is as much an art as it is a science. It is scientifically based, yes, but it's also quite intuitive. We have to weed through many clues as we work to determine which bits of information will help us to make a diagnosis and which are "red herrings," or clues that will lead us in the wrong direction. It is important to listen carefully and to be sensitive to the patient's mood. Does a patient seem reluctant to give information? Is she avoiding the question by giving extraneous information? Subtle messages need to be interpreted and deciphered. The doctor must then perform a precise examination that addresses all of the areas the clues point toward. This takes time, thought and energy.

Yes, I am tired at the end of the day.

Getting to Know You: Putting Patients at Ease

When I first meet a patient or his or her parent, I look them in the eye and introduce myself if we do not already know each other. Then, I wash my hands in front of them and shake their hands. I usually try to engage the younger child with a play on their name, a humorous comment or a little teasing. If a 6-year-old comes to the office for an illness, I might ask them why they've come.

If they answer, "Because I'm sick," I'll respond:

"I know you're 6, but why are you here?"

Many children this age cannot pronounce the number "6" very clearly, which means this round of questioning can go on for awhile, or at least until I see my charges losing patience, and then I let them in on the joke. Afterward, there is usually giggling.

With older children, I might casually talk about sports if they are wearing a uniform, or strike up a conversation about school or other activities. I do all of this to lighten the mood, then we move on to discussing the reason they've come to the doctor: the chief complaint. A routine checkup, a cough, sore throat, headache, vomiting or any other number of common or unusual complaints might bring them to my office. Some symptoms involve subjective complaints, such as pain, while others are more objective, such as a rash or a swollen knee. There is a whole protocol of questions I ask depending on the complaint and its complexity.

When I'm trying to learn more about a patient's pain, some questions I'll ask might include: Can you describe the pain? When did it start? What might have caused the pain? Where is it located? Does it radiate? Does anything make it better or worse? How intense is the pain? Does it interfere with activities?

When I'm dealing with younger children, I might show them pictures of different faces with a range of expressions from smiles to grimaces to tears and ask them to point to the appropriate facial expression. The most important thing is to pay attention to the patient's expression.

In order to doctor well, each physician must develop a persona with which he or she is comfortable and that he or she feels is effective in successfully interacting with and treating patients. This persona is unique to each doctor, and can evolve over a career. As the famous jazz musician Miles Davis once said, "Sometimes you have to play a long time to be able to play like yourself."

It can feel awkward for young physicians to treat patients who are older than they are. Because I was a pediatrician, this went double for me, as most of my patient's parents were older than I was. These people came to me for advice and assistance, and I needed to establish confidence in that relationship. Today, some of my younger associates introduce themselves by their first name. Because my patients come to me with the expectation that I will be a source of wisdom and authority, I choose to introduce myself as Dr. Berkowitz. I also try to keep the relationship very professional, maintaining strict boundaries and limiting how much personal information I share. I rarely have social relationships with my patients or their families unless there is a connection outside of the office such as a friendship between our children or mutual involvement in an organization. As I've matured, I've became more relaxed, and although I still encourage the doctor-patient mystique, I joke with the parents and children and share personal anecdotes that I think might be helpful for the specific situation.

I work to maintain a relatively professional persona, but in the end, my pint-sized patients sometimes call the shots. One even decided to rechristen me as "Dr. HoHo." I found this nickname rather endearing, even after the patient's mother explained to me that it was an allusion to Santa Claus, presumably because of my white beard and "slight" paunch.

I wear a bow tie and use a rubber rooster reflex hammer, but both of these items serve a very practical function in my line of work. I had a campaign slogan in the hospital pertaining to reducing infections: "No ties or bow ties." Regular ties are more likely to touch patients and carry germs, and bow ties are harder targets for little boys to spray. I used to have a fuzzy lion or monkey around my stethoscope until I realized that those items potentially transmitted infections. My older patients still remember those animals.

When I look into young patients' ears, I'll sometimes tell them I'm looking for potatoes. One of my older teenagers once asked me after I examined his ears: "Did you see any potatoes?"

We both chuckled.

More than a Healthcare Worker: Learning to Listen and Empathize

What makes for a good physician-patient relationship? Scientific knowledge, yes, but also communication and empathy. There have been studies showing that the doctor usually interrupts within 20 to 30 seconds of a patient beginning to speak. In reality, this is unnecessary, as most patients will not talk for more than a minute or two before stopping. Empathy is a different ball of wax. Certain people just have this quality, and the patient knows instinctively that they care. Others may be much more reserved and not display their emotions readily.

The patient must also know the doctor is listening. It does not engender confidence in a patient if he or she has the impression that the doctor's mind is somewhere else, or if the doctor is constantly checking e-mail or text messages. The advent of EMR (electronic medical record keeping) has made this a bit more difficult, as a doctor must divide attention between the computer and the patient. When I'm taking notes, I must now work with my back to my patients and concentrate not only on them but also on clicking the correct buttons and ensuring that I don't miss any fields as I type.

In an article published in the *International Journal of Medical Informatics*, researcher Dr. Enid Montague discussed the finding that physicians spend about a third of their time with patients looking at the computer screen. She concluded that this could potentially result in the physician missing nonverbal cues and other subtler forms of communication. To quote Dr. Montague: "It's likely that the ability to listen, problem-solve and think creatively is not optimal when physicians' eyes are glued to the screen."

How can a doctor learn to empathize and to listen? By following the lead of his patients. "Anil" was an 18-month-old toddler of Indian descent. I first met his parents for a consult when he was 14 months old. They'd brought in Anil because he was failing to thrive. He was significantly below the average in weight and he was not achieving his developmental milestones. The family had recently moved to our area. Anil had been diagnosed with multiple food allergies by another doctor and he had previously been admitted to the hospital for vomiting and dehydration. He was on a severely restricted diet of breast milk and very limited foods. His parents and I spoke at length about the evolution of his symptoms and about his hospitalization and his diet. It was clear that the boy was malnourished.

I listened carefully as I spoke with Anil's parents, and his father gave me all the clues I needed to make a diagnosis. By dad's account, the boy's vomiting had begun after his parents started feeding him a baby food that the father discovered contained soy. (The father had figured this out by carefully reading all of the ingredients for each of the boy's jarred foods.) Anil's hospitalization for dehydration happened around the same time his brother had a stomach virus, so the cause was unlikely to have been allergies. Anil had been on milk products well before his weight started dropping, which made milk an unlikely suspect.

The first thing I did was put him on a milk toddler formula. One month later, I checked on his progress. Anil had gained one-and-a-half pounds. At a checkup three months later, I found he'd gained another four pounds. He was now running and developing well. We continued to add new things to his diet, leaving out soy, beans and nuts. Anil's depleted physical condition had been the result of his prior physician's inability to *hear* what the boy's father was telling him. This could have been because the physician didn't take the time to listen or because he or she had preconceived notions about the cause of the problem and did not want these beliefs disturbed.

When a physician communicates with patients it needs to be done in a manner that is appropriate to their level of understanding. If you don't work in the medical field, for example, the excessive use of medical jargon can be confusing. I often joke that lawyers and doctors have invented their own languages in order to justify their fees.

It is also important for a doctor to acknowledge the patient's problem. Even if the condition isn't serious, it isn't helpful to say, "Oh, it's nothing." If it were nothing, the patient wouldn't be there. I have been called many times by parents concerned because their children have developed additional signs of illness, such as fevers or rashes, after a doctor assured them the child was fine.

"How could this be?" they ask me. "My child was just seen and the doctor said there was nothing wrong."

This is not a great confidence-builder, even if the parent simply misunderstood what the physician was trying to say. Either way, the communication was neither transmitted nor received properly. The message should have been: Yes, your child is ill, but the condition isn't serious.

I cannot emphasize enough how important the doctor-patient relationship is to the healing process. I am not just a healthcare provider! I am a physician! I care for my patients; not my clients or my customers, and there is a certain sacredness to this relationship. After all, patients are much more likely to follow instructions if they believe their doctor cares about them. Consequently, they are more likely to have better outcomes. Of course, a physician's knowledge has to be well-founded. A young intern may think he knows it all, when in fact he or she knows either a lot about a little or a little about a lot. There's just so much to learn about so many illnesses. You have to know when you do not know and ask for help accordingly.

As Persian philosopher Omar Khayyam once said, "He who knows not and knows not that he knows not – he is a fool."

Tell Me Where It Hurts: The Examination and the Treatment Plan

Imagine for a moment that you are a young parent with several young children, one of whom is sick. You've brought the troop to the pediatrician's office and you are trying to concentrate on the doctor's instructions, but it isn't easy. The baby is crying because she's tired and hungry, and the 2-year-old is climbing the walls of the examining room, eager to explore the big world awaiting him. Meanwhile, the older kids are fighting over stickers or whatever else. If you were in this situation, how easy would it be for you to recall and follow the doctor's orders?

Keeping such scenarios in mind, and keeping in mind that medication errors are a leading cause of medical complications, when I examine a patient and then communicate a treatment plan, I always consider the ability of the patient or parent to absorb and remember the information. Studies show that patients remember about 30 percent of what the physician tells them, and it's really not all that surprising.

When I am satisfied that I have obtained all the information I need from a patient, I begin the physical examination. The first thing I do is let the patient know what's going to happen. I'll tell them that I'm going to look in their ears, eyes, nose and mouth, and I try to either reassure them that nothing will hurt or to warn them if something may be a little uncomfortable. I always let apprehensive patients know that I won't do anything painful without a fair warning. Painful surprises are not a great relationship-builder. It is important to develop trust with the patient. When my wife was a child and needed surgery, her mother told her she was taking her to buy shoes. Unfortunately for me, that resulted in my wife developing a lifelong shoe fetish. It also made her more anxious about subsequent visits to the doctor.

When I begin the examination, I try to start with areas that feel non-threatening to the patient. I often begin an examination of a younger child while the child is still in his or her parent's arms, which is often soothing. I might also listen to the heart and lungs, and try to save the more uncomfortable or frightening portions for the end of the exam. If a patient's ankle hurts, for example, I begin by examining the opposite ankle first, or other parts of the leg. If the patient's stomach hurts, I ask where the pain is located and save that area for the last.

Once I've performed the examination, during which I often ask additional questions, I need to evaluate all the information in order to try and make a presumptive diagnosis. If I need confirmation, I may order confirmatory tests or just observe the patient for a set period of time if the patient is not seriously ill and no immediate treatment is needed. Sometimes there is more than one possible diagnosis – called a differential diagnosis – and further testing may be necessary to identify the specific problem.

Once the diagnosis has been made, I present a treatment plan. Part of my job is to educate the patient about the likely cause of the problem as well as situations that could make it worse, steps they might take to improve the condition and what they can expect to happen during the course of the illness. The more informed the patient is, the less doubt and uncertainty he or she will have.

First, I verbally discuss the steps that need to be taken, including how to administer the medications at the correct dosage and time. Then I write everything down for the parents to take home. I can give the best advice in the world and recommend the most effective medications possible, but if the patient doesn't follow my prescription, the problem will just follow its natural course. *Medication does no good when it just sits on the shelf.*

How do I as a doctor get my patient to follow the guidance I offer? I can try to bully them by saying: "I'm the doctor, so do as I tell you. I know what's right." Experience has demonstrated that this approach doesn't work. Trust and mutual respect are essential.

My wife, Kathleen, and I were once involved in a research study run by the American Academy of Pediatrics that examined obesity in children. We attended a two-day symposium on an interviewing and treatment technique called brief motivational interviewing, or BMI. This technique focuses on skillfully directing a patient or parent to describe the problem as well as their concerns and any potential remedies they can think of. The doctor lets the patient talk about the problem, but also encourages him or her to reflect on perceived obstacles to treating that problem. This requires the important quality of good listening skills.

A doctor might ask the mother of an overweight child, for example, to explain why the family eats fast food three times a week. The doctor might learn that she is a single parent who is rushing home from work and then must get her child to a baseball game within a narrow time window. Fast food is certainly one solution to such a problem, although it's not a healthy one.

The doctor can then simply remain silent for several seconds, during which time the mom might have an epiphany.

"You know, doc, they also have salads with grilled chicken on the menu," she might say. "Oh, and the supermarket right near my house just set up some tables! Maybe we could sit down for some fresh veggies and a quick, healthy main course."

More silence might follow, after which the doctor might reflect with the parent on the situation, acknowledging its difficulty but not letting her off the hook. The doctor might also ask the parent what other options come to mind. It is important to have the patient and parent, or even better their entire family, invested in the choices being made.

When discussing lifestyle changes that may improve a patient's health, the simplest (but not the most effective) approach is to narrate a litany of helpful actions. When I encounter an overweight child and his mother, I could rattle off countless suggestions: "Be more active, spend less time on the screen, avoid fast food, soda and juice drinks, have smaller portion sizes, make healthier food choices, eat more fruits and vegetables."

This is all very good advice, but to me the approach seems a bit overwhelming and impersonal. How will they even know where to start? A far better tactic is to examine the patient's lifestyle and to pinpoint the areas requiring the most radical adjustments. Do the parent and patient see these behaviors as a problem? If they do, the doctor can guide them to choose one or two actions that are feasible and that they are actually willing to perform. Together, doctor and patient can discuss a goal and select lifestyle modifications that feel practical and doable.

Take, for instance, a discussion about "screen time," or the number of hours each day a child spends staring into a computer or television or cell phone screen. Mom might say: "When I get home from work and picking up the kids from daycare, I take a deep breath, change out of my work clothes and start prepping dinner. The kids sit down in front of the TV. This time is a breather for us all."

This sounds reasonable, right? But what if these children are overweight and spend an average of three to four hours daily on the computer, in front of the TV or playing video games? A potential solution might be to have the children help prepare the dinner with age-appropriate contributions. I certainly wouldn't ask a 3-year-old to chop carrots, but he or she could easily get the carrots from the refrigerator while the older kids help with more complex tasks. This would carve out a bit of quality family time from an otherwise hectic day and encourage the children to feel more involved with dinnertime.

If the children are old enough and the conditions around the house are safe, I also encourage parents to send the kids outside to run around. Parents might also turn on music instead of television and encourage the children to dance or draw. A specific plan might be created with specific targets. Whenever changes are established to routine behavior, reluctance and apprehension are normal. The parent might even tell me: "That won't work with my kids."

In the end, the best choice is the one that works best for the whole family. If the parents or patient don't see their situation as a problem, my job is to help them to realize the benefits of taking action so that they are more willing to make the change. That is the first step, and for a family struggling with weight, it might involve revisiting the ravages that obesity has taken on the extended family: a father who died young from heart disease or a sibling who is struggling with diabetes. It might also involve revisiting an overweight parent's childhood and asking them to recall how they felt when they couldn't fit into fashionable clothes or were the last to be picked for a team because they ran so slowly.

Together we would then choose one or two lifestyle alterations and evaluate how well the changes are working with a follow-up visit a month later. If things are going well at that point, we might throw in a few more changes. If they aren't, we might try a different approach.

The BMI interviewing technique is well illustrated in a humorous, satirical novella by Calvin Trilling titled, *Tepper Isn't Going Out.*

Tepper is an ordinary man who likes to unwind by parking his car in a paid meter space in New York City and sitting there, despite the repeated protests of drivers searching for a free space. Tepper gains some notoriety when he stands up against city hall to preserve his right to park and simply sit and relax in the spaces for which he has paid. In the process he inadvertently becomes legendary for his ability to solve people's problems simply by sitting, saying little and listening to what they have to say. A little silence can truly go a long way.

Change also requires motivation. And motivation cannot be forced on a patient. It is particular to each individual. An asthmatic who is not very consistent with his meds might rethink this casual approach after he shows up in the emergency room in a panicked state, unable to breathe. A parent who was unconcerned about a child's weight might be ready to acknowledge the problem after an overweight sibling develops high blood pressure or has a stroke. However motivation comes, *it has to come from within.* Sometimes this requires an epiphany, or what experts in the field call an "Aha! Moment" in which a light bulb clicks on and a person suddenly says, "So that's what it's all about!"

My father smoked two to three packs of cigarettes daily for more than 25 years. One day he coughed up blood, and he grew terrified that he had cancer. A thorough evaluation fortunately came back negative for cancer, but he never picked up another cigarette. One of my aunts, on the other hand, was also a heavy smoker and developed heart disease requiring coronary bypass surgery, which was still then in its infancy. She had the surgery, was on the ventilator for days and spent about two weeks in the hospital. As soon as she got home, she started smoking again. She had two more bypass surgeries, but kept right on smoking. Interestingly, the ordeal did motivate her husband to successfully quit smoking.

It's hard to change habits, especially when the entire family is accustomed to them. When it comes to any kind of lifestyle change, it is ultimately the patient and/or the patient's family that has to do the hard part. Doctors can only guide, encourage and present the facts.

A Sacred Trust: The Importance of Confidentiality

I recently had an emergency consult with a young female college student. A friend of hers had called her parents to express concern about the girl's strange behavior at school. Her parents immediately picked her up from college and brought her to the office.

It was 5 p.m. on a Friday, and they sat in the waiting room while I interviewed their daughter. I asked her if she knew why she had been brought to me. She initially said "No," but quickly opened up to me about her depression and the circumstances contributing to her strange behavior. She was becoming more and more withdrawn and she was rarely leaving her room. She'd also begun to neglect her dress and eating habits.

After assessing her risk for suicide and determining that she had no serious inclination, I suggested that we talk with her parents about the situation. She was reluctant to do that because she didn't want to worry them, so I gave her a reality check. I asked her which situation she thought would be more worrisome to her parents: knowing that their daughter was struggling or being closed out entirely from her life.

She considered this new perspective, but remained wary of letting her parents know every detail of her situation. Together, we decided that it would be best to discuss her problems with her parents in as general of terms as she chose, asking only that they listened to what she had to say without prying too much into the details.

The young woman agreed that she needed to see a therapist. (Part of her despondency was related to the fact that her school had canceled an appointment she'd reluctantly and painfully made for a psychological evaluation.) We brought her parents into the room and together arranged for the family to make an appointment with a psychiatrist and for her to stay home with her parents until she was evaluated. It was a decision made by my patient, with my guidance. It was not forced upon her.

Confidentiality is a crucial consideration in the physician-patient relationship, especially when it comes to adolescents and young adult patients. As a parent and a pediatrician, I see both sides of this issue. Parents desire to have all possible information related to their child's health. Parents are also usually emotionally, financially and legally responsible for their children until they reach maturity, so they want to make sure that their children are taken care of properly. Physicians, on the other hand, place primacy on their relationships with patients. If a patient is to have optimal treatment for a condition, it is essential that he or she feels safe in sharing any and all health-related information. In certain situations, this requires the knowledge that a doctor will not reveal information the patient doesn't want shared. Breach of that agreement will destroy the physician-patient relationship. Of course, anything that endangers a patient's well-being or the well-being of another person must be discussed. Serious homicidal or suicidal intentions require notification to the proper people and authorities.

Handling the dilemma of confidentiality requires that the patient understand its primacy in our relationship. I encourage my young patients to discuss with their parents any part of their situation that the parents might need to know about to help the child maintain well-being. Most parents are supportive of their children, although there are situations in which the parents' and child's best interests are not in harmony. In that situation, my priority is my patient – the child.

The Only Constant: Navigating Changes in Technology and Medicine

"Kiernan" was born with a heart problem that rendered his chances of survival very low. His cardiac surgeons were able to creatively stabilize his condition, but there was no guarantee that he'd have a significantly long lifespan. And even if he did, he'd be destined to live a life compromised by heart failure, which would make any activity involving physical exertion extremely difficult. Unlike some of my previous patients, however, Kiernan was born in the age of heart transplants, and the heart of a 4-year-old killed in a motorcycle accident soon became available. At age 1, Kiernan received a new heart and the operation was a success.

Today, Kiernan has grown into a young man. He takes numerous medications to prevent his body from rejecting his transplanted heart and he has some residual disabilities from that initial period of living with a damaged heart unable to adequately deliver blood to his organs, but he's a happy, relatively well-functioning man.

Back when Kiernan was a baby, giving a heart transplant to a 1-year-old was a novel endeavor, and, like all scientific advances, it needed to be monitored for future complications. After 20 years, Kiernan developed some vague chest pain, which then developed into a mild heart attack. He had stents inserted into his coronary arteries and he was treated as any other older adult with a similar disorder would have been. Kiernan is again doing well, but he is still being monitored for any wrinkle in this new approach to treating his heart.

Four decades in private practice and encounters with patients like Kiernan have taught me something I couldn't have learned from a thousand medical textbooks or a hundred years in residency: humility. That humility developed as I began to realize that much of what I tell a patient that is considered to be standard medical knowledge will inevitably change later. As the Oath of Maimonides reminds us, the one thing that we can be sure of is change. There are relatively few additional absolutes. We work with the most accurate scientific information available, but knowledge bequeaths more knowledge. Humans, being inquisitive creatures, question all new information, and these constant challenges tease out both truth and fiction.

New treatments are monitored over time to determine their appropriateness and effectiveness. Sometimes, it isn't possible to determine these things until after hundreds of thousands of uses. All life is in constant flux, including people, society, and, yes, germs.

When penicillin was discovered, it was accepted as the panacea for all infectious diseases. During my childhood, I recall my doctor coming to my home because I had a high fever, examining me and then pulling out the dreaded syringe and needle for a penicillin injection in my rear end. At the time there was little downside to this approach. All disease-causing bacteria were initially sensitive to this antibiotic. Over time, though, bacteria became resistant to penicillin. New antibiotics were developed, with ultimately the same result. Today, we know that we must be more judicious in our use of antibiotics. Many antibiotic-resistant germs are causing diseases that are difficult or impossible to manage. When I began practicing medicine, we automatically treated all ear infections with antibiotics. Today, we prescribe antibiotics only for those infections most likely to benefit from their use. When the link to cholesterol and heart disease was uncovered, we switched non-breastfeeding babies to skim milk at the age of 1 month. Later studies emphasized the importance of fats for appropriate neurodevelopmental maturation. I can't attribute any specific instances of decreased intelligence to the use of skim milk, but today we continue either formula or breast milk until babies are 1 year old.

Our understanding of disease is also evolving. Asthma was once thought to be purely an illness in which the bronchial tubes went into spasm, which created breathing difficulty. We later learned that this condition has a strong inflammatory component, and this new knowledge resulted in a change in therapy. Treating this aspect of the disease appropriately resulted in far fewer deaths, fewer acute medical emergencies and a better quality of life for those living with asthma.

Arguments about the benefits of circumcision have gone back and forth over the last four decades. Current medical evidence favors newborn circumcision, as it reduces urinary infections in the newborn male and potentially reduces the risk of sexually transmitted infections and cancer of the penis in adult males. However, the current recommendations are constantly being reexamined.

The development of brand new diseases adds to our modesty. Back in the 1970s and early 1980s, a new phenomenon began cropping up at hospitals and doctors' offices across the world. Four or five days into a viral illness, commonly influenza or chicken pox, children were becoming increasingly listless, with some slipping into comas and even dying. I'd be called in to see patients who seemed to be improving from an ordinary viral illness but then regressed, becoming more lethargic and vomiting repeatedly. The symptoms were accompanied by an inflammation of both the liver and the brain.

This condition was first described in Australia, and it was soon named Reye's syndrome. Initially, all we pediatricians could do was support these children by trying to reduce the pressure buildup in the brain and hoping they recovered. It was soon determined that the syndrome was linked to aspirin use. Today, pediatricians no longer use aspirin for fever, and I have not seen a case of Reye's syndrome in more than 25 years.

Back in the early 1980s, we saw 4-year-old "Anna" in our office for what appeared to be a typical case of scarlet fever – simply strep throat with a rash due to a toxin produced by the bacteria. This is usually treated with antibiotics. Anna remained feverish and irritable and her rash continued to progress despite the administering of antibiotics, so we hospitalized her for further diagnosis and treatment.

That night, as was often my habit, I did a bit of bedtime reading. By that point, having been awakened over the years by numerous nighttime calls, I had developed a sleep disorder. I'd discovered that it was essential to be instantly alert during middle-of-the-night phone calls so that I'd be able to appropriately assess the situation. As a result, I'd become a very light sleeper.

I subsequently discovered that reading the American medical literature was the best technique for getting me to sleep. These articles were usually written in such a dull literary style that they had an unintended soporific effect. By contrast, the British medical journals, though often esoteric, were far more enjoyable to read.

That night, I encountered in my readings mention of a new disease, called Kawasaki disease. Patients suffering from the disease presented with prolonged fever, swollen lymph nodes, conjunctivitis (red eyes), dry lips, an unusual appearance of the tongue, swollen hands and feet with peeling from the tips of the nails, and a rash. The laboratory findings revealed an elevated white blood cell count and markers for inflammation as well as a subsequent rise in the platelet count. This illness was originally described in the late 1960s in Japan and then it was named after its founder. Kawasaki disease later migrated to Hawaii, then to the West Coast of the United States, and I began to suspect as I did my bedtime reading that night that it was now making its debut in Bergen County, New Jersey. I was right, and Anna proved to be one of the first cases in the area.

The major complication of this disease is the development of coronary aneurysms, which are balloon-like enlargements of the arteries to the heart. This can create heart problems later in life. We still don't know what causes Kawasaki disease, but we do know in most cases how to successfully manage the dangerous inflammation that can result from it.

Lyme disease, also a relatively new disease, was named after the place where it was first diagnosed: Lyme, Connecticut, but it soon spread further afield. I first encountered Lyme disease in an 8-year-old patient who simply had an increasingly severe headache and a low-grade fever over the course of a summer, without any prior signs or symptoms as far as we could see. It was only after I referred the case to an infectious disease consultant who happened to work in a geographical area with a high incidence of Lyme disease that the diagnosis was made. Our patient had Lyme meningitis, which was treated with four weeks of intravenous antibiotics that resulted in a complete cure. Today, that diagnosis would be routine. Chalk this one up to the changing environment, in which a human population surge resulted in an invasion of the deer's environment. People were then exposed to the deer tick, which is the vector in transmitting Lyme disease.

As a physician practicing in the 1980s, I was also witness to the rise of HIV and AIDS – the scourge of the decade. The cause was initially a great mystery. Numerous theories abounded, from God taking revenge on the gay population to immune reactions to sperm in the gut. Years of arduous research revealed the cause of HIV and AIDS to be a specific virus. The virus was initially considered a death sentence, but successful antiviral treatment has since been developed. The only HIV/AIDS patient that I treated was a foster child cared for by a parent in our practice, although one of my associates supervised an AIDS clinic in the inner city for a number of years before joining our practice.

Many unknowns remain. What role do pollutants play in disease? Links have been made between certain plastic byproducts and early sexual development in females as well as obesity. Certain environmental toxins are linked to the development of cancers. What effect does the decreasing ozone layer have on our health besides increasing the risk of skin cancers? It has been shown that ultraviolet light can cause genetic mutations in DNA. (I happened to write a paper in college about the mechanism for these changes.) It is conceivable that there are more insidious problems that will also be linked to this environmental disaster.

Consider, too, the effect of societal changes on disease. Accepted changes in attitudes and lifestyles have altered the traditional pattern of family life. Today, many women are electing to have children at a later age in life, and this is creating its own set of problems. With increasing parental age comes a higher risk of chromosomal problems in the offspring. There has also been a higher incidence of infertility, which has been mitigated by advances in medicine: increasing In Vitro fertilization as well as surrogate mothers and gestational carriers. Though they are for the most part highly successful, these techniques come with their own set of problems.

Does the increasing rate of autism relate to any or all of the aforementioned factors? It is well known that autism has a much higher association with certain genetic conditions, such as fragile X syndrome, which is the leading genetic cause of mental retardation in male children. It arises from an abnormally large number of repeats of a certain genetic pairing on the X chromosome. Will we find out that pollutants, UV exposure, advanced parental age or susceptibility to other environmental factors contribute to the rise in the number of cases of autism spectrum disorders? It is certainly possible.

Pediatricians work constantly to adapt to this changing environment, and we adjust our approaches to these new situations to best suit the needs of the children we treat. This is an evolving process. The rate of increase in scientific knowledge as well as the technological advances related to new surgical techniques, equipment and medications, along with their unforeseen consequences, tend to make our decisions a little less certain.

Part Two

How to Make a Human Being

IN PEDIATRICS, a physician has at least two patients: the child and his or her parent. Usually, the child is the easier to care for of the two. Parenting is no simple task!

So what does it mean to become a mom or a dad? An essential part of the survival of any species is reproduction, and humans are no exception. But we humans are complex, and the manner in which we choose to mate and reproduce is couched in emotion, tradition and culture. It's a complicated process.

For parents, the product of this union – a brand new life – symbolizes far more than just a means for mom and dad to perpetuate themselves in the next generation. Our offspring don't exist merely to sustain our genetic material; they also exist to sustain our culture and our values. We invest a great deal of emotion in our young to achieve this passing of the proverbial baton. Raising kids is an incredibly challenging commitment that can only be seen through to successful completion with a great deal of love, caring and guidance.

FOUR

Planning and Growing Your Family

THERE ARE MANY WAYS to make a family. I know this firsthand. After we lost our third fetus in a row to extreme prematurity 20 to 24 weeks into pregnancy, my wife, Kathleen, and I began exploring the possibility of adoption. (It was later determined that her miscarriages were the result of her exposure, while in her mother's womb, to DES, a hormone that was frequently given to mothers whose pregnancies were threatened. This treatment was later deemed ineffective and it was also found to be the cause of numerous complications, the worst being an inability to carry pregnancies to term and cancer of the vagina.)

Our adoption adventure began when my wife wrote a letter to a Colombian orphanage she'd heard about from a friend who had previously adopted a child. Kathleen mentioned the letter to me only in passing, as she wasn't expecting to hear back for at least six months. Ten days later, I received a call in my office from a Señora Canton. I remember the conversation vividly. I went into our x-ray room to pick up the call in private.

"Dr. Berkowitz," a woman's voice said, "I think we can help you."

I was confused until the fleeting memory of what my wife had mentioned about a week before flashed into my mind.

"Oh!" I replied.

"Yes, we have a baby boy for you," she said. "When can you come down?"

I was dumbfounded. I had no kind of plan whatsoever. Stuttering, I told Señora Canton that I needed to call my wife, and that we'd return her call that evening. I immediately called Kathy, who peppered me with a million questions. I had been in shock, unfortunately, and had not asked anything more than the essential questions. In addition, my waiting room was full and I had patients to attend to.

We returned Señora Canton's called that evening. My wife was much more eloquent than I had been. At that point, we had none of the necessary paperwork, which included an evaluation of our home and home-life plus an FBI clearance. This usually took months. As we were unfamiliar with the orphanage protocol, we wondered if they would hold the baby for us for that long. With the help of my father-in-law, who contacted his congressman, we were able to get all of this done in 10 days. Our first son was born Dec. 26, 1977. We left for Colombia to bring him home on Friday, Jan 13, 1978. A snowstorm had begun earlier in the day and we were the last flight out of John F. Kennedy International Airport in New York prior to its closure. Our flight had been delayed and we arrived in Colombia late that day, so we arranged to meet our son Henry the next day.

We arrived at the orphanage, Casa de la Madre y El Niño, the next morning. It was a simple brick building that was clean and very well cared for. Many of our fears were dispelled as soon as we entered this caring abode. We were brought to a private room, where we were introduced to our son for the first time. He was dressed in what I was later told was a white christening outfit. I can only say he looked angelic. Tears welled up in my eyes. Kathy was instantaneously reborn in that moment as a mother as she fell immediately in love with this little baby. He was our son. (I'll save all the details of this amazing experience for my next book.) Close to three years later, we contacted the orphanage again, and shortly afterward we were blessed with our second son, Noah.

Most people have preconceived notions and fantasies of the kind of family they'll eventually have, but reality might ultimately bear little resemblance to these idealized visions. You might have problems finding the right partner, or you might choose a same-sex partner. You or your partner might have difficulty becoming pregnant or carrying a pregnancy to term. Children may be born with disabilities or challenges, and family situations can change over time. Life offers up many combinations and permutations. When you are planning your family, the key is to keep an open mind.

The Most Complex Organism of All: Dissecting the Modern Family

Two families, both concerned about ADHD (attention deficit hyperactivity disorder), brought their children to my office. One family had come to me for advice after receiving a concerning call from the child's school. The child had been struggling in the classroom and was having difficulty concentrating. He also bounced off the walls at home, but this didn't ring any alarm bells for the parents, as this kind of behavior wasn't an important concern in the dynamic of this particular family.

The second family brought their child in because the child wasn't able to sit down quietly for their 30-minute dinners, although there were no issues at school. In this family, structure was paramount. Had the families been switched, I would have had one less patient visit me.

What works for one child and family may not work for another child, or even for a different child in the same family. This is related to the concept of "fit," or how a behavior within a family constellation is consistent with expectations. Those expectations, in turn, are determined by the spirit of the era in which a child grows up. Let's take what used to be considered the Traditional American Family. Picture The Cleavers from *Leave It to Beaver*, or Ozzie and Harriet Nelson from *The Adventures of Ozzie and Harriet*, both picture-perfect families of the 1950s and1960s. The husband worked and the wife was a stay-at-home-mom who ran the household. Dad would come home from work each evening and the family was there to greet him and sit down with him to a wonderful family dinner. They lived in the same community in which they'd probably been born. Family and friends were all around. Such a setup is now the exception rather than the rule.

After the Cleavers came the '60s: the era of sex, drugs and rock 'n' roll. Add to that the Women's Liberation Movement in addition to every other conceivable liberation movement. The next altering factor was economic relocation due to job mobility. Families went where the jobs were and moved whenever the company relocated or a parent switched jobs. The paradigm of lifetime employment in one company and a lifetime spent living in one town became a myth of a bygone era, and it also often became essential for both parents to work in order for them to comfortably raise a family.

There has additionally been an increase in the divorce rate. At first, divorced children lived with their moms and had a father that was involved only if they were lucky. Then, fathers and mothers began remarrying and sometimes having children with their new spouses. Now, 50 years out from *Leave It to Beaver*, a "typical" family situation could consist of a child living with his/her mother or father, plus the spouse's previous child and a new baby who is the product of this second union. I call this situation "His, Hers and Ours," and you can also add a variety of other configurations to this modern family smorgasbord: adopted children, gay parents, surrogate moms, gestational carriers and sperm and egg donors. These new and increasingly complex family setups have the potential to lead to very complex family dynamics.

Some families function on the inviolable concept of blood, and the connection by blood relationship supersedes almost everything else. There can be verbal and even physical abuse. The family is still paramount. In other families, a wrong word, a misperceived look or, more commonly, a disagreement over money, can destroy the family integrity permanently.

Most families have at least one skeleton in the closet. Pat Conroy, one of my favorite authors, has written very eloquently about the complexities of the family. In the memoir, *The Death of Santini: The Story of a Father and His Son*, Conroy describes his interactions with his dying mother and abusive father. He writes:

> Not a single family finds itself exempt from that one haunted casualty who suffered irreparable damage in the crucible they entered at birth. Where some children can emerge from conditions of soul-killing abuse and manage to make their lives something of worth and value, others can't limp away from the hurts and gleanings time decanted for them in flawed beakers of memory … There is one crazy that belongs to each of us … The variations are endless and fascinating.

A revolutionary change in the concept of parenthood occurred with the birth of a little girl named Louise Brown on July 25, 1978. She was a 5-pound, 12-ounce baby born via planned cesarean section at Oldham

General Hospital in England. Her parents had been unable to conceive for nine years due to the mother's blocked fallopian tubes. That mother, Lesley Brown, underwent a procedure that later became known as IVF, or In Vitro fertilization. The embryo was grown in a petri dish and then implanted into the mother's womb, and Louise Brown became the world's first "Test Tube Baby."

As my own adopted boys got older, my wife and I needed to figure out how to explain their adoptions to them. Suggestions were all over the map. Some authorities suggested lying to the children: you were their biological parents. Unfortunately, there were many situations in which this had backfired and totally undermined the trust between child and parent. Others joined adoption organizations that held regular meetings and proudly proclaimed to the world that their children were adopted. We took the middle ground. Their adoptions were a fact of their lives, not a defining characteristic. We were honest with our children and answered any questions they had truthfully. We neither advertised nor hid the fact that they had been adopted. One son wanted to know if we got him at Bloomingdale's, an upscale department store. The other son had little interest. Our first son had a strong attachment to the fact that he was Colombian. Our second son would not discuss it. We did not push this information down their throats. We tried to respond to their cues, and we provided any information they desired.

Aside from my personal familiarity with the age-old practice of adoption, my first significant experience with an unconventional family occurred about 25 years ago when I met in my practice a lesbian couple that had decided to have a child. One of the moms was inseminated with the sperm of a male friend and they had a little boy. They were both very attentive to this child, but eventually the moms separated and one of them moved away. They both continued to be involved with the boy, but just one mom became the primary caretaker. We lost touch with the family when the child was about 4 years old and his primary mother had to relocate for a job. As this was an uncommon situation in that era, I have always wondered how the boy turned out.

More recently, I met "The Blandas," a family made up of a gay male couple and two children conceived with the sperm of one partner and the help of a surrogate mom. The result was an adorable set of twins: one girl and one boy. They are now both in school. Even more recently came "Mrs. Mayle," a 48-year-old mother of two girls who encouraged her husband to agree to have another child later in life. (The older sisters were preteens by this time.) Prior to examining the new baby girl, I reviewed the medical records and then I asked the nurses to check the results of the blood type test. I figured there had to be some mistake, as the baby's blood type could not have been derived from this biological mother. I then discovered, hidden in the chart, a new piece of information: the embryo was not biologically this woman's, nor was it her husband's. The embryo had been the product of the union of a sperm and egg donor grown In Vitro and implanted into this older mom. The pregnancy had been very difficult and the baby was delivered by c-section. Today, that baby is a healthy girl who looks remarkably similar to her two other sisters.

In my practice, I also encountered "Mr. Paul," a successful alpha male who could only be described as a serial marrier. Every 15 to 20 years, he would trade in his former wife for a newer model, and with each new marriage came new children. Our practice has taken care of all his children and even some of his grandchildren. He seems to be a very affable man. I don't know what the dynamics of his family are, but I know that he tries to keep all of his children connected. It is unusual and intriguing to consider that the youngest of his children are the uncles, 20 years younger, of the offspring of his oldest children.

At a recent checkup for an adorable 9-year-old girl, I encountered another interesting setup. When I was asking the mom about the child's social history, I was told that the child was living with the mom, grandma and maternal aunt. I asked if the father was involved only to be told that there was no father. The mother was a single mom who had conceived by artificial insemination using donor sperm. She was struggling to figure out what to tell her child. This was an epiphany to me. How do you inform your child that they are the product of someone else's sperm and/or egg, grown in a test tube and then implanted into a "mother's" uterus, or in this case, the product of the mother's egg and donor sperm? Or what if it was your parents' egg and sperm implanted into another woman's fertile uterus? The possible combinations are endless.

This mother took an interesting approach. Through doing research on the Internet, she was able to locate other women in similar situations. She was even able to find a group of moms who had been inseminated by the same donor sperm. They contacted each other by punching in the group number that identified their "Sperm Donor Family." Some of these moms exchanged names and photos of their children, some of whom bore striking resemblances to each other. They even tried to have a reunion, but all of the 31 offspring from this donor were spread throughout the country. Some of the moms formed a de facto support group for the purpose of discussing various circumstances unique to their situation in addition to establishing a connection between these biological sibs.

Brave New World is here.

The First Child Is like the First Pancake: Seasoning Your Parental Frying Pan

Welcome to parenthood. However you've managed to arrange it, a new and totally helpless creature has now arrived. And all rational thought leaves your brain. When you have a baby it is as if as your brain dies, or as one of my patients put it, when they remove the placenta, some of your brain goes with it. The center of the universe has shifted, and life as you knew it ceases to exist. You are now a captive to this heir or heiress to the throne, and as you are further charged with the task of preparing this creation to assume all the duties of the kingdom in a regal manner, you need to do everything perfectly ... Wrong!

Relax. The wonder of childhood is its freshness. Everything for the infant is a new experience. Having a new baby is one of the most exciting experiences a person can have in life. It is also one of the most horrifying. The joy of bringing new life into this world is a wonder – and an overwhelming responsibility. This becomes more apparent every day in our fluid society, where families are often broken up by divorce or geographical separation. The support of a caring, attentive parent brings reassurance to a child even if he or she doesn't parent perfectly. After all, new parents somehow survived their own imperfect childhoods, didn't they?

What happens with the first child? They are the trailblazers. Every breath is an adventure. Every burp is a success. Every coo is brilliant. Each milestone is a new frontier, from nursery school through adolescence, to college and beyond: the first romance, the driving test, the first job and then later, possibly marriage and kids – your grandkids. The first child brings with him a novelty that doesn't exist with siblings born afterward. When the first baby does not wake up on time for his feeding, the parents check to see if he is breathing. When this happens with subsequent children, the parents breathe a sigh of relief and enjoy a little more rest or perhaps take some time to catch up on neglected duties or pleasures.

So how is the first child like the first pancake? Think of it this way: the frying pan is never quite the right temperature the first go-round, and the first pancake is invariably flawed as a result. But there is an upside. Although the pan is not fully seasoned, that first pancake gets by far the most attention. Perhaps this is why, historically, first children are often the most neurotic but also the highest achievers among their siblings.

When parents feel sorry for a child due to his or her specific birth order, I remind them that every position in the family has its advantages and its disadvantages. The first-born gets the most attention. The middle child can get lost in the shuffle, but she can learn from older siblings while also dominating younger siblings. Younger children may get less direct supervision, but down the ladder there is also more independence.

Children often regress when a new sibling enters the mix. They may become more infantile, belligerent or even aggressive. I also remind new parents struggling with this issue that the older child actually needs more attention than the new baby. If the parents have any leftover energy, they should put it toward spending time with the older sibling when he or she is behaving well rather than only when he or she is misbehaving. Family and friends can also assist in giving the older child extra attention, which will allow the child to feel special while minimizing any resentment. In numerous instances, grandparents or aunts and uncles have come to the aid of the new parents by showering the older child with companionship and arranging activities with them such as taking them out to their favorite place for lunch. Positive reinforcement is far and away the most productive technique for mitigating jealousy in an older sibling.

A mother of one of my patients illustrated the birth order scenario perfectly with a little vignette of her own: when her first child dropped a bagel on the floor, she picked it up, threw it out and gave him a new bagel. When the second child dropped a bagel on the floor she wiped it off and handed it to her. When the third child dropped her bagel on the floor, the mom just kicked it back to her.

Sit back and enjoy the excitement of this being discovering his feet for the first time, or the thrill of her first yelp. Your reactions will reinforce these new behaviors. Even for a pediatrician, the wonder of observing a child's unabashed excitement over the littlest things never ceases, whether it's an infant's reaction to being given a tongue depressor or an older child's thrill at receiving a sticker. There is no conflict in this joy, although as the children get older, they often become more selective in their choice of stickers. To the pickiest of these kids, some moms will say, "You get what you get, and don't get upset."

Even then, the rudest youngsters excepting, I offer a choice of two or three different stickers. Before we started giving stickers to the children as a reward for surviving their examinations, I used to draw faces on the wooden sticks we used to examine throats. I continued to be amazed at how disappointed many of the children were if I forgot to give them that little gift. (Of course, in this case, I'd immediately right the error by making one of these "stick figures.")

Children make you old but they keep you young. The worrying and the responsibility wears you out, yes, but kids' excitement and wonder keep you from aging too much. And as they grow, you benefit from being exposed to the youthful ideas and energy of your children and their young friends.

Humans give birth to adorable, helpless creatures, and this dependency feeds into many parents' (usually moms') nurturing instincts. However, some parents are petrified by the neediness of this new being. If you find yourself in that position, ramp up your support system, be it family, friends or enrollment in a parenting class. If you find these feelings paralyzing, you may be suffering from postpartum depression, which can be very serious. It is important to make your physician aware of your symptoms so that you can receive the appropriate therapy.

When Families Change: Helping Children Understand Divorce

According to the American Psychological Association, the divorce rate in the U.S. is at about 40-50 percent for first marriages, and it's even higher for subsequent marriages. It's not an understatement to say that the majority of modern American families will be touched in some way by this difficult event.

Divorce is often an emotionally traumatic event for all members of the family, and some resulting degree of hostility between the separating parents is the rule rather than the exception. That said, it's important to remember that for a child, any single event such as a divorce is far less catastrophic than being subjected to the trauma of ongoing negative interactions between parents.

Let's consider two extreme examples culled from my practice. "Mr. and Mrs. A" realized that they were no longer compatible. They were raising three children together, but they had decided it was best at that point to separate and divorce. They were financially comfortable and had worked out mutually acceptable agreements that made provisions for child support, living arrangements and shared responsibilities. They had explained the reasons for their divorce to their children, reassured them of their continued love for them, and they were working hard to act civilly toward each other.

Now consider "Mr. and Mrs. B." They were married for several years and were unable to have their own children, so they adopted an adorable little girl of about 1-and-a-half years. When the girl turned 4, the mother accused the father of sexually abusing the child. Up to that point, I had seen no indication in either the child's or the father's behavior that suggested this. The mother and child were separated from the father until the investigation was completed, and the mother initiated divorce proceedings. The father was only allowed limited supervised visits with the child, although the investigation concluded that there was no evidence that he'd sexually abused his daughter. Joint custody was awarded to both parents. Rather than submit to the court order, the mother illegally fled the state. Legal proceedings ensued. I never learned what happened next, but I'm sure that the situation had a devastating effect on the child.

There's no doubt that divorce has an impact on the children in any family. This doesn't mean that it's preferable to expose them to the hostility and conflict of a very unhappy marriage, especially because they may misunderstand their role in the drama and assign themselves some of the blame.

The effect of divorce on children varies depending on the stage of childhood. Children under the age of 3 are unable to understand the meaning of divorce, but they certainly react to the grief and anxiety of their parents and may exhibit irritability, increased crying and separation anxiety. They may also become aggressive, develop sleep disorders and stomach problems or display developmental regression. Some children additionally become more babyish and needy. Children older than age 4 may also blame themselves for the current situation by wondering how the situation might be different if only they'd been "better" children. School performance may diminish and nightmares may increase.

If the divorce occurs when the child is in early adolescence, he or she may suffer from self-esteem problems. The disruption of the child's idealized family can also make it more difficult for him or her to trust others, and the anger and confusion caused by the perceived betrayal can be detrimental to the development of close relationships. Depression, aggressive and delinquent behavior, decreased school performance, inappropriate sexual behavior and problems in the development of emotional self- sufficiency can all be an effect of divorce.

Under any circumstances, children will experience divorce as a significant loss, but none of the problems outlined above is inevitable. The best divorce outcomes occur when there is minimal disruption to the child's routine, a continued demonstration of love by the parents, adequate support and even psychotherapy, if needed.

What is the role of the pediatrician in this process? We need to be attuned to any of the aforementioned mood or behavior disturbances that might indicate familial discord. When a child whose parents are divorcing comes for a visit, it is important for the pediatrician to question the parent and child about stressors in the family, and to pay attention not only to the child's words, but also to his or her mood and body language.

It is also vital to emphasize to the parents how important it is for them to demonstrate their love for their children during this time. The process of and reasons for the divorce need to be explained at an age-appropriate level to minimize the guilt the child often feels, and routines and disciplinary structures should be maintained as much as possible. The parents need to be made aware of the potential reactions that their child may have to the divorce. And parents must be reminded above all that the worst thing they can do is to use the children as weapons against each other. The child's love for each parent should not be compromised or infringed upon in any way. As pediatricians, we also need to remind the parents that we won't be taking sides. We are not marriage counselors, but advocates for the child, and we are there to offer advice that will ease the transition.

FIVE

Newborns

WHEN OUR DAUGHTER-IN-LAW was celebrating her first
Mother's Day after the birth of her daughter – our granddaughter Eliana
– my wife discovered a beautiful poem. The Indian mystic Rajneesh
wrote it, and it sums up perfectly the transformation that occurs with
the birth of a child:

> The moment a child is born, the mother is also born.
> She never existed before. The woman existed, but the mother,
> never.
> A mother is something absolutely new.

What is definitely true for any new parent – mother or father – is that
life as you know it has just changed forever. There is life B.C. (Before

Children) and life A.C. (After Children). Nothing can totally prepare you for the responsibility of caring for a helpless newborn, which is a being totally dependent on you for its existence. Birth can confound some of the most intelligent people in the world. People whose professions carry great responsibility and who are able to read and then follow the most complicated manuals in existence are left dumbfounded by it. Take a deep breath, though: If it were so hard, there wouldn't be billions of people on this earth.

Confounded, Dumbfounded and Smitten: Your Baby's First Days

What happens when a baby is born? My obstetrical colleague, Ronald Allen, MD, would always warn mothers as their babies were preparing to enter the world that they would come out bloody, wet and blue – not the most appetizing sight for the uninitiated. The appearance of the baby at birth can even be a little frightening if the parents are unaware of what to expect.

Another associate, Michelle Mayer, MD, tells new mothers that despite all the training she had as a pediatrician, which exposed her to many medical conditions including the newborn intensive care unit and newborn resuscitation, the first two weeks after her first delivery were the hardest of her life. She even had her mother stay with her as a support for the entire first week.

So what's a brand new parent to do? There is no definitive answer. As they say in the movie *Parenthood*: you need a license to own a dog. You need a license to drive a car. But you don't need a license to have a kid. There are thousands of books about how to "properly" raise children, and many offer conflicting opinions. At best, these are rough guides, and at worst, they are just plain confusing, because being a parent requires on-the-job training. Every baby is different, born with a unique temperament and responding differently to similar stimuli. This means that we need to listen to our children.

The first month is called the "Newborn Period." Think of it as relocating from a heated, indoor swimming pool where you are being fed intravenously to a big, cold ocean where you must breathe your own air and sing for your supper. Not an easy transition.

The cascade of events that occur to hasten this transition, beginning with the very first breath, is amazing. The fluid-filled lungs need to learn to breathe air. The baby has to regulate its own body temperature in a changing environment. Connections have to be closed so that blood is directed to the previously fluid-filled lungs, which now feed oxygen to the body and away from the maternal placenta, from which the baby has been disconnected. This process, which begins with the first cry after delivery, is usually satisfactorily completed by 4 weeks of age. In essence, the baby at this age is functioning at a very primitive level. The baby sees and hears, but the brain has a limited ability to process the incoming information. When I was a neophyte physician it was even believed that the newborn baby was blind, although we subsequently discovered that newborns exhibit preference when looking at patterns and faces and might even recognize the mother's voice, having been exposed to its pattern while in the womb. At this early stage, the baby is a creature of instinctual needs: food, warmth, sleep and cleanliness; and parents respond with their own set of instincts. The love we have for our progeny is a bonus, and this love is partially a product of the hopes, dreams and fantasies we have for our offspring.

The 72- to 96-hour period immediately after birth is an extremely crucial time. The initial weight loss common for most newborns starts to reverse. It is also during this time that certain abnormal conditions reveal themselves. Physiologic jaundice, which is part of the normal process of the recycling of blood, causes 30 percent of newborns to develop a yellow tinge to their eyes and skin. The condition usually stabilizes. Jaundice due to abnormal causes, however, may get worse. Most dramatic of all is the presentation of certain forms of congenital heart disease abnormalities in the formation of the newborn heart. The usual processes of closure of the fetal connections that directed blood away from embryonic lungs to its life source, the placenta, is an essential part of the normal developmental process. However, for infants born with certain heart conditions, these connections need to be maintained to ensure survival. This is why pediatricians recommend a follow-up visit for all babies discharged from the hospital before day four.

"Karl" was a strapping and beautiful 10-pound, 7-ounce baby boy born without complication. Had he survived, he would have been about 40 years old today. At 72 hours old, Karl started to feed less vigorously and he soon became pale and mottled. It turned out that Karl had hypoplastic left heart syndrome. In this syndrome, the left ventricle, which is the pumping chamber of the heart, is underdeveloped. As those primitive connections between the left and right circulatory systems began to close after birth, Karl's inadequate pumping chamber became unable to sustain him. He went into heart failure and emergency measures were performed to reverse the closing of these openings. A surgical shunt was made for Karl to ensure the patency of these life-sustaining but usually unnecessary fetal connections. Imaginative surgeons had designed all kinds of procedures to improve the function of hearts such as Karl's, but these hearts were never normal. Karl lived a sedentary life and required medications to strengthen the pumping of the heart and to rid his body of the extra fluid accumulated by its inadequate functioning. He struggled with his weight, which was a family characteristic, and this put extra strain on his already weakened heart. He succumbed in his early 20s. Had heart transplants been available at the time, he'd probably still be alive.

One recent night, I received a call from a disheartened mom who was concerned about her 3-month-old, who had previously been sleeping through the night. Mom had read a book by a doctor who insisted that parents take away a baby's pacifier at 3 months. The parents had done so and were now struggling with the baby's newfound sleeplessness. This was a major problem, as the father had to go to work each morning and the mom was attending school. I reminded them that anyone could write a book, *even someone like me.* There was no scientific or developmental reason why at 3 months she automatically had to "pull the plug." I directed the parents to give the pacifier back to the baby. I never heard from them again about the issue, and by the next checkup, the baby was back to her prior sleeping patterns.

Many parents worry about the implications of a pacifier or thumb-sucking in a newborn. Initially, sucking is an instinctual behavior. This behavior is different from the habitual thumb-sucking of an older child. In infancy, it is a soothing action, and I prefer that a baby use its thumb or fingers to a pacifier. If the pacifier falls out at night, the parent needs to get up and replace it, whereas a baby can simply put her own fingers back in her mouth. In most cases, the need for instinctual sucking extinguishes itself.

New parents quickly learn that babies cry because they can't speak. A parent must learn the meaning of each cry based on the sound and the context of the cry: "I'm tired" sounds different from "I'm hot or hungry," and "I'm wet or dirty" sounds different from "I just want to be held."

You can't spoil your new baby. They are creatures of instinctual needs. There will be plenty of time to worry about spoiling them when they are older. You should never be afraid to hold your young infant for fear of coddling them; being held is very soothing and makes a baby feel more secure. He or she will probably also cry less in the long run.

Remember, too, that unrealistic expectations can lead to unnecessary frustration. Parents of newborns are invariably exhausted, as most babies wake up repeatedly during the night for feedings. The young infant's stomach may not have the capacity to hold enough food to sustain it through an extended period, and a baby's rapid growth requires an almost-constant energy source. The neonate usually doubles his or her weight by 4 to 5 months and triples that weight within a year. Often, a parent is advised by a family member or friend to feed solids to the small infant in order to allow him or her to sleep through the night. This usually doesn't work until the child is ready. It is a gift any time a child sleeps through the night before the age of 6 months.

Some parents read every book on pregnancy and childhood they can find and become totally confused by the different philosophies of the different authorities. Which one is right? Just as with diet books, if there were one right answer, there would not be thousands of these books.

All in all, most children in developed countries can and do survive to adulthood. This wasn't always the case. As recently as the early 20th century, 50 percent of children died by the age of 5. Most of these deaths were the result of infectious diseases, many of which are now preventable. One of our main jobs as pediatricians is to keep the baby safe, which ensures the best chance for a long and healthy life. Two of our most important additional goals are accident prevention and immunization. By exercising these two practices, parents increase the odds of raising their children successfully into adulthood.

An Immunological Safety Belt: The Case for Vaccinating

Prior to the institution of the universal Hepatitis B vaccination, I examined a 7-month-old Chinese girl who had been fussy over the course of several days. This was her family's first office visit, and their history was unremarkable. A physical examination revealed a fussy and lethargic infant who was severely jaundiced (yellow). I immediately admitted her to the hospital, where testing revealed that she had an overwhelming liver inflammation caused by the Hepatitis B virus. She became comatose, was transferred to a regional intensive care unit and subsequently died. Upon further investigation, it was discovered that her mother was an asymptomatic carrier for Hepatitis B and had unknowingly passed it on to her newborn child. The incubation period for this virus is up to six months, meaning the disease may present itself up to half a year after exposure. Hepatitis B is endemic in many East Asian countries, with many adults unknowingly carrying the virus. This meant that a female carrier could pass the virus on to a newborn infant, with grave repercussions.

Today, all pregnant women are tested for Hepatitis B. Because it is most often passed to the baby during the birth process, being aware of the condition ahead of time allows for doctors to ensure effective preventive treatment at birth. It was also determined that the Hepatitis B virus that resided undetected in adults led to a much higher incidence of liver cancers in this population. In effect, then, the Hepatitis B vaccine, when given to children, became the first anti-cancer vaccine.

Over the course of my career, I've witnessed cyclically occurring reports of this complication from this vaccine and that consequence from that vaccine. They've ranged from seizure disorders to multiple sclerosis, with the most troubling concern being a possible link between vaccination and autism spectrum disorders. Studies have repeatedly refuted any direct association between vaccines and any of these conditions. Recently, a massive study at Babies' Hospital in New York put aside any relationship between the MMR (measles-mumps-rubella) vaccine and autism. Prior research had revealed that thimerosal, a mercury preservative previously used in vaccine manufacture, also likely has no role.

Still, apprehension exists in the minds of many parents. To simplify the reasoning behind the autism-vaccination claim, parents of autistic children will tell you that their child was totally fine before he or she was vaccinated. But just because there is a coincidence in the timing of the symptom with the timing of the vaccine does not mean there is a cause-and-effect relationship. As it turns out, speech starts to develop exponentially after 15 months of age. Often, parents' attention will be called to their offspring's problems at that point because the child's speech development is aberrant and often delayed. What occurred in the toddler's recent past? Voila, the MMR! So that must be the cause. Yes, the vaccine did precede the parent's *awareness* of the problem. But that may be coincidence. Recent research has revealed brain abnormalities that can be spotted soon after birth in many children who later develop autism. The cause is not the MMR. The timing is coincidental, and this coincidence is the reason for parental concern.

The overemphasis of the dangers of vaccines is in part a product of our success in eradicating many of the worst childhood diseases. I can tell you what might happen if not enough children are vaccinated because I've seen it happen before. Prior to the first administering of the polio vaccine in the early 1950s, there were more than 50,000 cases of paralytic polio yearly in the United States. I was among the first groups of children to be immunized against polio in school. Parents were so relieved by the availability of this immunization against the scourge of polio that long lines of children anxiously awaiting their vaccinations were a common sight. Everyone had a friend or a relative who had been debilitated by this disease, which didn't even spare the President of the United States of America, Franklin Delano Roosevelt.

Up to five percent of infants who developed whooping cough in the first year of life also used to die. Three out of every 1,000 cases of measles caused either death or brain damage and at least 50 percent of pregnant women who developed German measles early in pregnancy either lost their babies or delivered a child ravaged by heart, brain, hearing or visual defects, or possibly all of them at once.

Over the years there have been many examples of the destructive power of false claims against vaccines. In the 1960s, concern in Japan about the MMR vaccine led to a sharp decrease in immunization for these diseases. Within 10 years, epidemics broke out anew, along with all the concurrent complications. In the 1970s, celebrity British physician Gordon Stewart, MD, questioned the value of the DPT (diphtheria-per-tussis-tetanus) vaccine and proposed on television, radio and in print that immunization be abandoned. Again, there was a sharp decline in immunization rates, which was followed by an astronomical increase in cases of pertussis. In 1977 there were 99,000 cases of whooping cough, which led to 23 deaths, mostly in infants.

Our modern hesitation to vaccinate is also in part a product of the success of these anti-vaccination campaigns. We rarely see the ravages of these diseases because we rarely see epidemics. Many of us have reservations about complications from immunizations. Let's consider the trajectory of the polio vaccine immunization program, which well illustrates the pediatrician's dilemma with regards to vaccine safety: The initial polio vaccine was the killed-virus injectable Salk vaccine. This was later supplanted by the live oral Sabin vaccine, which was a more effective vaccine, especially when it came to controlling epidemics. But there was one concern about the live vaccine: VAPP, or vaccine-associated paralytic polio, which occurred at a yearly rate of four to eight cases. About 50 percent of those cases occurred in caretakers, many of whom were immune-suppressed. Because of these very few cases, the entire polio vaccine program was shifted back to the killed, injectable vaccine, despite the fact that it was less effective.

Certainly, there is a risk involved in everything you do. Just driving in a car results in more than 30,000 deaths each year in the United States according to the National Highway Traffic Safety Administration, but do we think about that when we start the car and opt not to drive our kids anywhere instead? No. We purchase cars with features designed to keep us safe in case of an accident, because we know that most of the deaths and serious injuries involving children are the result of the child not wearing a seatbelt. Initial vaccines are like seat belts – the front line of defense – while subsequent vaccines are like the front and side airbags and other safety features installed in the body of a car. Some of these safety features may have less of an impact than the belts, but they still reduce injuries and death.

Everything that you do or do not do has its consequences, and the benefit of immunizing your child far outweighs any risks. Committing the sin of omission when it comes to vaccines will leave your child susceptible to potentially serious diseases.

Nourishing Your Baby: Is Breast always Best?

I recently encountered a new mom who was devastated because she required a cesarean section in order to deliver a healthy baby. She was most upset not about needing the surgery, but about the fact that her newborn wasn't able to experience the voyage through the birth canal. Initially, there were also some worries about her ability to nurse exclusively because the baby was small and losing too much weight. She needed an endless amount of reassurance to convince her that she was not a failure. With support, she was eventually able to nourish her child solely with breast milk and to forgive herself for denying her child the pleasure of a vaginal birth.

There is no question that under ideal circumstances, nursing a baby will provide nourishment and beneficial immunity to the baby and warmth and comfort to the mother. But breast-feeding is not a religion. Many babies have been successfully raised on infant formula. When I was born, it was considered a status symbol to feed one's baby formula, while breastfeeding was reserved for those who were unable to afford to bottle-feed. If it works for both the mother and the child, I encourage nursing without reservation. However, if the baby is not thriving or the mother is uncomfortable physically or emotionally with breastfeeding even after seeking out all possible nursing support, other options must be considered. A mother who is anxious or in discomfort while breastfeeding passes that tension on to her baby, who may become fretful and aggravate the problem.

Some breastfeeding groups tend to make mothers who are unwilling or unable to nurse feel inadequate. Keep in mind that a healthy and happy baby is not healthy and happy simply because he or she had an ideal life. Mothers and fathers will be imperfect and most children will survive. The newborn baby needs above all to be fed, clothed, changed and loved.

Where, How Long and with Whom? Deciding on Childcare

The ideal environment for infants and children is in their home with their primary caregiver, which has historically been the mother. A baby does not need multiple activities and significant social interaction with peers. What's most important for a baby developmentally is a consistent, warm and responsive relationship with a primary adult caretaker. A tender interaction with soothing speech and positive reinforcement for any of the baby's responses is optimum for growth. This bonding forms the foundation for the child's security. Computers or television absolutely cannot replace it.

To reiterate, this is the *ideal* environment. Unfortunately, life isn't always ideal, and this setup is only possible if the parents are willing and able to provide it. These days, many families require both parents to be income producers. Even if this is not required, some parents enjoy or need their professions. People often define themselves by their professions and feel empty or incomplete without them. If a parent is going to give up his or her profession only to become resentful and/or financially stressed, then it is no longer an "ideal" situation. My feeling in this case is that less is more. Being able to keep the baby at home in a familiar environment with a trustworthy relative or nanny is the best alternative. The next best alternative would be having the baby cared for by a responsible adult, preferably licensed in childcare, with one or several other children.

After I'd been in practice about 10 years, there was a drop in the pregnancy rate. Young people were waiting longer to get married or to develop serious relationships and to have babies. Many were deciding to have fewer progeny, and some opted to have none at all. This decision was made on the basis of lifestyle or finances. Many young adults were fearful of the responsibility of raising a child. The old family structure in which parents, children and extended family all lived in proximity to each other was disintegrating. Under the prior circumstances, you were not alone raising your child, and that framework offered new parents a great sense of support. In addition, the cost of raising children had risen exponentially. The result of all of this was that we pediatricians were seeing fewer newborn babies as patients. Simultaneously, daycares began to expand, and the reduced number of healthy checkups was more than offset by an increasing number of sick visits, particularly in the younger children.

Daycare is a necessary evil, but even the best daycares, with beautiful, sanitary environments and warm and capable staff are incubators for infection. Infants and toddlers are immunologically incomplete. Their immunity is supplemented by antibodies transferred from the mother during pregnancy, which start to decrease after birth. This decrease is mitigated to a degree by immune factors provided during breast-feeding. Babies are also "immunologically naive," having lived for nine months in a sterile environment, unexposed to any of the millions of viruses and bacteria that populate our world along with us. The greater the early exposure to multiple snotty infants and toddlers, the more often a child will become sick. To give you an idea of the impact daycare has had, consider this: When I was finishing my residency and starting my practice, fever in infants was so unusual that every febrile baby under 5 months of age was *automatically* admitted to the hospital over concern for a serious infection. Now only febrile babies under 1 month old are automatically admitted.

This exposure is not all bad. After the first two years of being sick every other week, particularly in the winter, your child has been exposed to most common germs and has developed significant immunity. Pre-kindergarten and early grade school are often smooth sailing after this.

Newborn Illnesses in Context: When to Call Your Doctor

One of the most important medical decisions a parent makes is the decision of whether or not to call the doctor when an injury or illness occurs. For some parents, the threshold for calling is very high, while for others any worry merits a call. I will not list a litany of conditions necessitating contact, as this would be onerous, boring and has already been done, besides. (Many pediatric practices have this advice available on their websites.) But a few basic concepts are helpful in guiding you when the question of whether or not to call your doctor arises.

Foremost, if you have any concern that your child is in imminent danger, call the 9-1-1 emergency number first and your pediatrician second. Situations indicating imminent danger include: loss of consciousness lasting longer than a second or so, extreme difficulty breathing, persistent convulsions or increasing unresponsiveness. If any of these conditions are recurrent, it's also a good idea to have a treatment plan intact before calling 9-1-1.

Another concept important to understand is that the more immature the child, the less likely you will be able to identify what is wrong. I have had many infant patients whose only symptoms were a prolonged cough or a prolonged cold come into the office with blazing ear infections. Symptoms can also be deceptive. I recently saw a 1-year-old for her checkup, and mom was concerned about an ear infection because her daughter was constantly touching her ears. After examining the ears and determining that they were clear, I explained to the mother that infants have a hard time localizing pain, and that ear touching can relate to any discomfort in the mouth, including teething. To complicate matters more, the discovery of the ears as a new part of the baby's body leads the baby to constantly revisit this appendage until it is no longer novel.

Infants can't tell you what they are feeling. Urinary tract infections may manifest themselves as only fever, while ear infections may be accompanied with vomiting. Serious, life-threatening infections may present without any fever at all. In general, any infant fewer than 3 months old with a fever greater than 100.5 degrees Fahrenheit (38 degrees Celsius) merits a call to the doctor.

Remember also to put things in context. The urgency of an illness is dictated more by the appearance of your child than by any actual sign or symptom. A child who has a 103-degree temperature and is running around is of less concern than a child who has no fever and is listless. A child who has intermittent tummy aches but is active between, and has his usual appetite without vomiting or diarrhea, is not imminently concerning, although a call may still be warranted.

Attention is also merited when an illness doesn't follow its normal course. A cold that is worsening after four to five days or lingering for more than 10 to 14 days may indicate a secondary bacterial infection. Fever that lasts more than three days raises concern for a disease process other than the typical virus. A child who does not improve after 48 hours from the start of antibiotic treatment also merits attention. Persistent vomiting, particularly with diarrhea and the onset of lethargy and decreased urination, suggests dehydration.

In short, look at your child before you panic, and don't hesitate to seek an outside opinion. A caring physician is available to respond to all reasonable concerns, and we learn to expect more calls for little babies, especially from first-time parents. When in doubt, make the call.

SIX

Infancy

THE PERIOD FROM 3 TO 9 MONTHS OF AGE in a baby's
life is what I call "The Honeymoon Period." Babies of this age are adorable, and aside from possibly not sleeping through the night, they are
little trouble. Many first-time parents start thinking about trying for a
second. Wait! Once your child becomes mobile, there is no rest except
for when he or she is sleeping or confined to a safe area. Toddlers have
boundless energy and like to creep, crawl, climb and put everything in
their mouths. Infants are far simpler.

What Happens Next? Your Quickly Changing Baby

Over the next few months of life, your baby will become more responsive to external stimuli. She coos and smiles, looks around and starts

reaching for things. The infant also gains more control of her muscles. This development progresses from the head downward, with neck and head control followed by control of the arms, and later, the legs. The baby starts reaching and grasping before crawling and walking.

Meaningful interaction between the baby and her mother (or primary caretaker) begins at about one month with the social smile. This differs from earlier smiles, which I call "smiling at the angels" because they have no relationship to the external world, but rather to an internal satisfaction such as having the tummy filled or enjoying a sweet sleep. The parents' positive response to these actions encourages more expansive displays. Next, we see cooing and even laughing. There are few things as enchanting as the belly laugh of a 5- or 6-month-old while you are tickling his tummy.

Subsequently, the baby develops more and more motor control. The infant starts to reach for things, initially in an uneven manner. Eventually, she is able to grab items first by raking them in with the fingers and later by using the pincer grasp – thumb and forefinger – to pick up small objects. The baby also begins to sit steadily, which allows her to start feeding herself.

Parents are often quite anxious for the day to arrive when their infants and toddlers start to crawl, walk and talk. In truth, the most parent-friendly baby accomplishments are sleeping through the night and, if the child is bottle-fed, learning to hold a bottle. You have to be careful what you so anxiously wish for, as those wishes often come back to bite you in the behind. The child that you couldn't wait to hear say his or her first words now won't stop talking, and you're constantly running after the child who only yesterday you found yourself wishing would start to crawl.

One of the most exciting events for parents in the life of an infant is the introduction of foods. I was recently asked by the parents of a young child who was solely breastfed: "When can we introduce foods? We heard from our relatives that the baby will sleep longer when we do."

The baby was 4 months old and in the top percentiles in weight, which was assurance of adequate nourishment. I prefaced what I said next by warning the parents that only 50 percent of what I was about to tell them would turn out to be correct. I discussed the misconception that introducing foods early on would increase nighttime sleeping. I discussed the current philosophy about holding off on solids until 5 to 6 months of age in babies who were exclusively breastfed. Next, I elaborated on the circular route that theories of feeding had taken over the course of my career, from advice to start skim milk and cereals at 1 month to advice to selectively avoid certain foods until a child had reached 2 years. This latter approach, along with the idea of limiting the choice of foods introduced until the first year, was promulgated by the belief that the early introduction of "foreign" proteins would increase the development of allergies, including asthma. As this practice continued, however, we in fact saw more and more asthma and food allergies. Recent studies now show that earlier introduction of the most highly allergenic foods, specifically nuts and fish and possibly eggs and milk, actually reduce the incidence of subsequent food allergy and possibly asthma (although this is not the sole factor).

So what's the *correct* answer? I can only present the current recommendations in the context of years of experience. One of the advantages of such experience is that it allows one to develop some perspective. You see trends come and go and you come to understand that there is a bit of leeway built into most of these medical guidelines. There is room for individualization. If a 3-month-old has maxed out on formula and becomes increasingly hungry, I'll tell the parents that they can start cereals. One of my dictums is that I don't worry about fat babies or skinny kids, assuming that the child is not fed *every* time he or she cries. For the most part, if children are healthy, I worry about skinny babies and fat kids. Obesity in a child is only a possible indicator of adult obesity after the age of 3.

Crib or Torture Chamber: Traversing the Complicated Terrain of Bedtime

When my wife and I had our first child after experiencing a number of pregnancy losses, we were captives to this cute miracle of life. At around age 2, our son became difficult to put to sleep. One night, we were entertaining some friends for dinner and listening to him cry in his bedroom, our stomachs in knots. We went up to soothe him and as soon as we left he started crying again. It was at that time that our friends, who happened to be European, urged us to let him cry himself to sleep – sleep which he badly needed.

"You are not torturing him," they told us. "He is torturing you."

I pass on this same wisdom to parents who struggle with similar sleep issues. Of course, certain parental behaviors are more likely to lead to these issues. One such behavior is allowing your infant to fall asleep at the breast or bottle. Infants should be put in their cribs as they are getting drowsy but before they actually fall asleep. Babies do often wake up, and they need to learn to fall back to sleep without a nipple in their mouth.

Co-sleeping, or sleeping in the same bed with your infant or toddler, is not only dangerous but also encourages sleep disorders. That said, co-sleeping is a necessary fact of life in certain family situations in which there are multiple children and limited space or resources. It is also more prevalent in certain cultures. Recently, during a baby's 9-Month Checkup, I inquired about the infant's sleep. The mom complained that her child was waking up multiple times during the night. I asked her how she handled the situation, and she told me she responded by bringing the baby into her bed. This isn't an uncommon response. Co-sleeping may be more convenient for mothers who are breastfeeding, particularly in the case of young infants, as it reduces the need for mom to get out of bed to nurse. The downside is that it puts the baby at risk of suffocation, especially when it comes to fledgling babies whose small size and lack of mobility make them vulnerable to smothering. Suffocation can occur when a parent rolls over on top of the infant while in a deep sleep or when the baby is accidentally smothered in a soft mattress, pillow or covers. Psychological studies have also implicated co-sleeping with a delay in individuation of the baby and difficulty separating from the parent.

Feeding or playing with your older infant or toddler if she awakens at night incentivizes a maladaptive behavior. If the baby awakens and the parents play with her or feed her, she will look forward to rejoining the party the next night. If as a child I were given milk and cookies each time I woke up, I, too, would eagerly anticipate my next awakening.

To parents who have a young child over the age of 6 months with a sleep disorder, I offer the following advice: You can either use the Ferber Technique or the Berkowitz Technique. Richard Ferber, MD, achieved acclaim for writing the book *Solve Your Child's Sleep Problems*, which outlined his system for desensitizing a child to a parent's absence during sleep by having the parents leave the child's room and return at gradually increasing intervals. His technique was fairly successful when properly applied.

I, on the other hand, didn't write a book (until now). The Berkowitz Technique is too basic: It is simply to let the child cry. The provisos are that you do not intervene and the child is not acutely ill. The child may cry for two hours the first night. Subsequent nights will result in gradually decreasing periods of crying. But if you go in after a period of crying, the child will realize the tactic of prolonged crying is effective and this will result in longer periods of crying until either parent or child prevails. Does my "heartless" tactic permanently scar the infant? Recent studies suggest that it doesn't.

Sleep is essential for babies. A tired child is a cranky child. There is now evidence that tired children also have a higher incidence of obesity and can have difficulty concentrating in school. Sleeplessness can even be confused with ADHD (attention deficit hyperactivity disorder). It is essential that your child develop healthy sleep habits beginning in infancy.

... But is that Normal? Evaluating Your Baby's Development

To know what is abnormal you need to know what is normal. One book I relied on while preparing for private practice was *The Normal Child: Some Problems of the Early Years and their Treatment*, written by Ronald S. Illingworth, MD, an illustrious English pediatrician. The photographic plate opposite the title page depicted a woman breastfeeding twins, holding one in each arm in a football hold. That picture, worth a thousand words, was an awakening for a neophyte pediatrician: I was busy visualizing a host of preconceived theoretical ideas about parenthood, but that image branded onto my mind the starker, day-to-day realities of life with children.

I spent countless hours in medical school learning about what constitutes a normal physical exam and what the normal developmental milestones are for children at each stage and age. And there have been many instances in which a mother has brought her child to me, concerned because her older child had performed a certain behavior at an earlier age, or because another sibling was bigger or smaller at the same age. What it is important to understand is that "normal" is a range. A random sample of two or three children, which is the usual number of children in a family, is not sufficient to determine what is normal. You need hundreds of children for an accurate assessment of what is normal for a specific age.

When I was a young teenager, I knew two brothers, "Ira" and "Jeffrey." I was astonished at the differences between them. Ira, the older brother, was skinny and small. Jeffrey was two years younger but he was significantly taller and broader. How could a "younger, little brother" be bigger than his "older, big brother"? It ran counterintuitive to my thinking. My own sons were also quite different. One son lost his first tooth at age 4, while the other son didn't lose his first tooth until 6-and-a-half years of age. One was potty-trained by age 2, while the other waited until 3-and-a-half years of age.

When should you become concerned because a child is not yet walking or putting words together or potty-training? Large studies have been done that have included follow-up examinations years later in an attempt to pinpoint what constitutes a "meaningful delay" for most of these developmental tasks. A child who is not walking by 18 months or putting two to three words together by 24 months may be in danger of having an underlying neurological problem that needs remediation to minimize or avoid a long-term deficiency. When they are significant, these delays put the child at risk for continued delayed development, which may require intervention in order for the child to achieve his or her maximum potential. These meaningful delays are the ones that must be acted upon, and in many cases they require a referral to health services or specialists. But, again, "normal" is a range.

The most essential truth for new parents to grasp is that children are not little adults. They are evolving human beings. The ultimate product will be an adult person, but until that point there are significant physiologic, physical and mental differences. There are not only size differences in children versus adults, but also differences of proportion. The younger the child, the proportionately larger his or her head will be. The function of certain organs such as the kidneys is initially incomplete. These factors have a significant effect on treatments. The most challenging differences are in the neurocognitive areas. A baby's ability to process information and control her voluntary muscle movements is very limited. The process develops slowly over time and varies from child to child.

A human baby who has no concept of anything other than herself transforms over many years into, hopefully, a responsible member of society. The usual evolution occurs in stages depending on the maturation of the brain and nervous system and is modified by parental input. The process of learning to see oneself as something other than the center of the universe develops over time as the infant grows into a toddler and then a child. Throughout this process, he learns that his needs and wants may not always be satisfied immediately, or even at all.

Unfortunately, a number of people, diagnosed as narcissists, will never outgrow this self-centered belief system. The child who can get everything he wants by having a tantrum or whining, or the child whose every effort is glorified even when it's mediocre, might well develop a distorted view of things. He is unlikely to understand that the outside world doesn't share his perspectives, and he's unlikely to accept the fact that the sun, the moon and the stars might not rise and set around him.

We see the ultimate results of a self-oriented worldview all around us. Consider politicians or celebrities caught up in scandals. Their first response is usually to blame someone else. If that doesn't work, they may make some half-hearted, face-saving apology that really doesn't address the bad behavior or acknowledge responsibility. Take, for example, baseball great Alex Rodriguez, who refuses to acknowledge that he might have taken performance-enhancing drugs, despite all the evidence stacked up against him. Or consider those Wall Street execs who brazenly manipulated the banking system, or the stereotypical teenage star behaving badly. They view the world solely through their two eyes and seem unable to consider any other point of view.

SEVEN

Toddlerhood

AH, TODDLERHOOD. This phase of childhood is often called "The Terrible Twos," but some babies also experience Terrible Ones or Terrible Threes. Some kids are just terrible! They might have difficult temperaments or they might have an underlying medical disorder that makes them uncomfortable. I had a patient, "Megan," who was a terrible 1-, 2- *and* 3-year-old. Her mother even joked about trading her in. Then, all of a sudden, at 3 years of age, it was as if a switch had been turned on. Megan became the most delightful child, and later even worked summers in our office before she eventually became a nurse. Keep the faith.

Big Head, Short Temper: Understanding the Toddler Body and Mind

The period between 9 months and 2 years of age constitutes toddlerhood. During this period, the baby wanders further and further from his parents, often coming back for reassurance and periods of clinginess, as he ventures farther out into the world and begins to make connections. Children of this age struggle for independence yet are still totally dependent. A 2-year-old might not know exactly what he wants, but this doesn't stop him from stubbornly advocating for his desires. Think of the 2-year-old who insists on going out to the park on a cold winter day without a coat only to start crying moments after he steps into the freezing air, or the child who is cranky, exhausted and rubbing her eyes but spiritedly fights your efforts to put her to bed.

Teething is a fundamental milestone for babies in this age group. On average, the first teeth appear between 5 and 7 months. Babies can start teething months before the first teeth erupt, and often, we see babies mouthing everything and drooling by four months of age. There is a debate as to whether this indicates the beginning of teething or if it is just the start of the oral stage, in which babies use their mouths as a significant sensory organ. I believe they are probably teething, but really what difference does it make? I have seen first teeth appear as early as birth and as late as 2 years of age. There is usually a specific order of eruption for teeth, starting at the middle and moving back, and beginning with the lower gums and proceeding to the upper gums, but I have seen many variations on this. When I see an infant whose first upper teeth are not the central incisors (the middle two) but teeth to the left and right, I tease the parents that their tiny "vampire" will grow into a little devil. Almost without exception, if the child has hair and nails, the teeth will arrive.

If parents are in anguish over a delay in the appearance of teeth, I remind them that the later the teeth come in, the less time they have to decay. There are many myths about teething. In reality, teething can cause discomfort, low-grade fevers (fevers below 101 degrees), some runny noses and a slight looseness of stool. Teething does not cause high fevers, cough, vomiting or diarrhea.

Another defining precept of toddlerhood: the fundamental job of the toddler is to rule the universe. The world is out there for the taking, and as children's author John J. Plomp reminds us, the only thing children wear out faster than shoes are parents. Toddlers are exploratory, and they'll investigate everything from electrical connections to their own body parts. Any interruption of this activity is unwelcome. A parents' main goal is to protect the toddler against dangers and also to provide a structure that allows for appropriate rest and nourishment without inhibiting natural curiosity. I often hear parents express concern about their toddler's preoccupation with their sexual organs, to which I reply: "Children 18 months to 5 years of age only have one hand. The other one is down their diaper." As long as the child is discreetly performing this activity, nothing needs to be done.

One important process that occurs as a baby develops from a newborn into a 2-year-old is that he or she learns to grasp the concept of object constancy. From birth until about 6 months of age, the baby views everything as a part of herself. She's hungry and the breast appears. She needs to be held and arms reach out to hold her. At some point between 6 and 9 months of age, the baby becomes aware that the breast and arms that nurse her and hold her are not a part of her. When that body of constancy is not available, for all intents and purposes, it does not exist, and this creates separation anxiety. Babies between 6 and 18 months have selective anxiety differentiating between their mothers and everyone else, sometimes including their fathers. We call this stranger anxiety, and it demonstrates that at this point in development, the infant has come to comprehend the uniqueness of her mother or primary caregiver.

The next developmental leap occurs when the child is able to understand that an object can exist even if she cannot see it. Games such as peek-a-boo reinforce this awareness. The subsequent step in the evolution of this skill set is for the child to be able to search for an object she does not see. This requires the acquisition of mobility, which also evolves between 6 and 18 months of age. The last part of this process involves developing the ability to associate an object with a word or a symbol. When children are able to do this, they only need to picture the word or symbol in their minds to conceive of its existence. This accomplishment requires a certain degree of neurodevelopmental maturation.

Three Things You Can Never Make Them Do: Communicating with Toddlers

Let's review a typical conversation with a 2-year-old:

"Let's get dressed."

"No!"

"Why not?"

"No want to!"

"If you don't get dressed, then we can't go outside."

"No!"

"Mommy would really like you to let her put your clothes on!"

"NO!!!"

It seems that most of the average 2-year-old's vocabulary has been replaced by two letters: "N" and "O."

So how does one deal with this kind of encounter? First off, don't argue with a 2-year-old. Babies of this age need to feel independent. State what you'd like your child to do, and if there is opposition, offer acceptable choices. Put out several outfits, for example, and ask your child to choose one. If all else fails, you must simply dress your child under protest. Remember: you are the parent and arguing all day over getting dressed is not a constructive use of anyone's time. After the battle over getting dressed, a new fight could arise over eating lunch, or taking a nap, or brushing teeth. It goes on and on and on, so choose which battles you really want to fight. Do not make issues to prove a point. You can let your 2-year-old win if it is not important. In the end, it's probably a good thing that 2-year-olds are so cute – it may be crucial to their survival.

When it comes to toddlers, the wisest words ever conveyed to me came from my senior partner, Alan Benstock MD, who noted: "You can't make them eat, sleep or go to the bathroom." That sounds pretty scary. So what *can* you do? Well, you do have some control. You can decide what time to put your child to bed, you can select the variety of foods you offer him and you can encourage him to go to the bathroom. I do not know of many 2-year-olds who will actually starve themselves. And as long as their parents are toilet-trained, healthy children will eventually be potty-trained as well. Trying to force them to train is a lose-lose situation. The child loses the self-esteem that he could have gained if he'd acquired the skill on his own terms. Often, children who feel forced to train may start to withhold bowel movements, which can lead to constipation, pain with defecation and fear of going to the potty.

There are several clues that indicate a child is getting ready to train. The initial part of the equation is communication. The child needs to verbalize or in other ways transmit to the parent the need and desire to go to the bathroom. The child must also be able to discriminate between the sensations of fullness of the bladder and fullness of the bowels. And lastly, the child has to develop control over the muscles that initiate and control the flow of stool and urine. Often one of the first signs that a child is getting ready to advance is that he will begin to dislike the sensation of a dirty diaper. Remember that the ability to interpret these sensations and to master muscle control requires neurodevelopmental maturation, the course of which varies with each child.

Imagine, besides, the conflict a toddler feels upon discovering that the product of all this potty training and the result of all of the encouragement and praise, the bowel movement, is treated with such total disdain and then flushed unceremoniously down the toilet. How strange!

Acquiring control of excretory functions is a great achievement for both the child and parents, but it might come at an unexpected time. After all the encouragement that we gave to our son to potty train, he saved his first bowel movement in the potty for his babysitter. What a disappointment that was for his parents! Mastering this skill brings a child the pride and self-assurance needed to prepare to master other tasks. Children who are physically or mentally coerced lose out on this morale booster.

Bumps, Bruises and Sudden Cracks: Dealing with Accidents and Injuries

Once, my son Henry was watching *Sesame Street* while he ate a snack. My wife, Kathleen, was in the other room. All of a sudden, she heard a loud cracking noise. She ran into the den to find him holding a hammer. There was a crack in our television, which was one of those big vacuum tube TVs. She pulled him away and called the television repairman, who warned her to stay away from the set until he could rush over. It was a dangerous situation, as the TV could implode. When we asked our son why he'd taken the hammer to the TV, he said that he had wanted to meet Ernie, one of the main characters on the show. Children of this age interpret the world through complex thought processes that may confound adults. My son's toddler brain was incapable of understanding the difference between the image of a character and the character himself.

It takes just a split second of distraction or preoccupation with one's other children for something to go wrong. The majority of the time, the child survives without complication. When a child is injured due to an oversight on the part of the parents, their remorse is overwhelming, even if there is little or no damage. I often tell them: "This is why we call them 'accidents.'"

Of course, there are times when such accidents turn disastrous, as with a 2-year-old patient of mine who drowned while he was with his 5-year-old sister and his mother stepped away momentarily, or with another 2-year-old who climbed a chest of drawers and had the furniture fall down on him and break his neck. In yet another tragic case I encountered, a grandmother was backing up her car in a parking lot, did not see her small grandchild behind the car, and struck him. The child subsequently died. For every horrific injury or death, however, there are probably hundreds of near misses. The lesson: as a caretaker you need to be alert and careful.

Keep in mind, also, that it is as important to be lucky as it is to be good. Many years ago, my 4-year-old son was playing in his room with a friend from nursery school. My wife heard a big thud and ran upstairs. Our son was crying, "Mommy, mommy, Jay's dead!" My wife looked into the room and saw a pair of feet, apparently not moving, protruding from under an armoire.

She called out, "Jay! Jay!" and when she got no answer, Kathleen exerted superhuman strength and lifted up the armoire, only to find Jay scared but unharmed, his head and neck fitted nicely into a cutout in the top of the cabinet. In retrospect we can laugh, as it reminded my wife of the Wicked Witch of the West in *The Wizard of Oz*, whose shoes were the only part of her remaining after she melted.

Another example: My wife was cooking dinner one afternoon while my almost-4-year-old son played in the playroom alone with his 10-month-old brother. Kathleen felt a degree of safety because the baby was confined to a playpen. All of a sudden she heard the patter of little feet behind her in the kitchen. It turned out Henry had cut Noah out of his mesh safety net. Noah could easily have scooted out the door or climbed the steps only to fall backwards and severely injure himself. Instead he chose to find his mother.

Aside from adolescence, I consider toddlerhood the most dangerous time when it comes to the potential for accidents. Toddlers have no sense of danger, they are clumsy and they put everything in their mouths. They need to be protected against all potential hazards. This is best done by childproofing the surrounding environment with an eye for preventing falls, burns, drowning, choking and poisoning.

Firearms also require the utmost vigilance when a toddler is in the house. Parents who believe their toddlers are "too young" to know where a parent's gun is located may be in for a tragic wake-up call. Some years ago, before the current rash of mass shootings began, I recall a number of incidences in which small children who were playing with their parents' guns accidentally discharged the weapons and killed other children. The American Academy of Pediatrics recommends storing guns outside of the home. This is the most effective method of reducing gun-related catastrophes. If you do decide to keep guns and ammunition in the house, they should be locked away. This is the second-most effective way to reduce gun-related accidents.

When more minor disasters such as accidents and tumbles do strike, remember that toddlers simply aren't tall enough to seriously hurt themselves by falling from their own heights. The knowledgeable pediatrician John Samson, MD, imparted this bit of wisdom to me while I was doing a rotation at Children's Hospital Los Angeles. (He wasn't referring to minor injuries such as bruises and cuts, which are par for the course with toddlers.)

When toddlers fall, they come down head-first because of their incoordination and the disproportionately large size of their heads compared to the rest of their bodies. However, they do not have the mass or the height to generate enough force to inflict on themselves serious injuries such as concussions. This knowledge ought to be some comfort to parents who watch their toddlers continually falling and hitting their heads while they are learning to walk. All bets are off, of course, if a child falls from an elevated height. (I recently Googled Dr. Samson and located him at his office. I told him I'd rotated through Children's Hospital Los Angeles more than 40 years ago, and that I was fairly sure that he was the attending physician who had imparted this useful wisdom to me. He told me it had, indeed, been him, and that he was still in pediatric practice after 48 years. It was a very exciting call.)

Basketball Player or Jockey: Predicting Your Child's Growth

When a child reaches 2 or 2-and-a-half years of age, many parents have the same question: "Can you predict a child's ultimate height? My mother or grandmother told me you can just double their height at this age."

Sometimes this is true, but most of the time there is no correlation. There are many formulas in existence that purport to predict height. One is to average the parents' heights and add two-and-a-half inches for a boy or subtract two-and-a-half inches for a girl. This is contingent on many factors, including an average age for puberty. There are many variables. Obviously, if you have two tall parents who produce a tall 2-and-a-half-year-old boy, he will most likely grow up to be taller than average. But even this may not be the case, as there may be a family member who is short who happens to pass on his or her genes. There are also early bloomers who are tall as children but stop growing early, or late bloomers who are short in high school but continue to grow late into adolescence and ultimately reach average or even above-average height. So much for that myth.

At checkups, the pediatrician plots height and weight on a growth chart, which compares the child to other children of the same age and also demonstrates the toddler's growth pattern. The chart helps doctors and parents to see if a child is keeping up with his or her prior growth pattern. This is important because sometimes the first indication of a serious illness can be a drop-off in growth, weight and/or height. A typical growth pattern from age 2-and-a-half to around puberty is two inches and four pounds per year. Other factors may also come into play in determining ultimate height. What has historically been the case for families immigrating to the United States, for example, is that the height of offspring increases for the next two generations.

In the end, a child has the best chance of achieving her maximum potential height if she is adequately nourished and gets enough sleep.

Grist for the Mill: How Much Intellectual Stimulation Is Enough?

There is an old joke about a child who would say absolutely nothing despite the dedication and concern of his mother. Then, because of a death in the family, the mother had to leave the child alone with a babysitter, who served the child a frozen dinner to eat. When he saw the meal, the child blurted out: "Why are you serving me this crap?"

When the mother returned and heard that the child had spoken, she grew very excited and asked him, "Why are you suddenly able to speak?"

To this, the child replied: "Until now, I had nothing to complain about."

Child development is not a steady process. The brain's connections (the synapses) can develop in fits and starts. All of a sudden, a child who has said nothing is talking in full phrases, or a child who hasn't even crawled is running. It seems as if the switch is turned on only after that final electrical connection is made. During the first two years of a child's life, what is most important is a constant and nurturing figure who interacts with and reads to the child. Over the following years, the child must slowly acquire social skills, adapt to a structured environment and be gradually introduced to educational materials in a fun way.

The necessity of teaching computer skills, a second language, or any other formal educational programs to infants and young toddlers has not been proven. I do, however, recommend that parents who speak another language use that language as the main language in their home, as it will promote the development of language skills in their children. The children *will* learn the language of their country of residence, as that is the language they'll be exposed to in school, on the radio, on television and through most other forms of outside communication. Being constantly exposed to two or more languages may cause a slight delay in speech development, as there may be some confusion in the brain with the acquisition of more than one language. This is temporary. Studies now show that what a child gains is the increased ability to develop language skills in later life.

EIGHT

Childhood

ONCE, I WAS TALKING WITH MY YOUNG SON and he said something that struck me as startlingly brilliant and insightful. So I asked him, "How did you know that?"

His reply: "My brain told me."

The integration of so many disparate parts into a whole person is just beginning in early childhood. Impulses that the toddler views as unacceptable to his parents may now be externalized into imaginary people who exist outside his body. These imaginary characters become responsible for any disagreeable impulsive thoughts or actions. It is not until around age 5 or 6 that the child can incorporate these unacceptable thoughts into a conscience. This conscience becomes an internal control mechanism used to subconsciously modify behavior without the outside threat of a disapproving parental figure.

Hello, Motor-Mouth: Talk, Coordination and Interaction in Early Childhood

Between 2 and 4 years of age, the child also experiences an explosion in the rate of skill acquisition. Motor-wise, children become much more agile. Their language skills multiply geometrically. Whereas a 2-year-old may be able to put two and three words together, a 4-year-old can express her thoughts clearly and in coherent sentences. Socially, children shift from non-interaction with other babies to parallel play, in which they watch another child to learn what others are doing. Finally, they move to interactive play. During this kind of play, children must determine some rules and learn to share.

This development can vary between boys and girls. Little girls are like mature, albeit very diminutive, little ladies, while little boys are emotionally much more underdeveloped and generally less evolved. One of the funniest scenes to observe is to watch a two-and-a-half-foot-tall girl give a detailed dissertation of her day's activities while a little boy of the same age in the same room is busy playing with his cars and trucks, uttering nothing but, "Rrr! Rrr! Rrr!"

The next step in development used to be referred to as the Oedipal stage. Oedipus was a mythological Greek king who unknowingly killed his father and married his mother. Dr. Sigmund Freud, the father of present-day psychiatry, coined the name for this period of childhood. Freud was a late-19th and early-20th century physician who crystallized the concepts that things always aren't what they seem and that people struggle with subconscious fears and desires. He named this period the Oedipal stage for the presumed struggles boys have at this age with giving up their sexual desire for their mothers and their resentment against their prime competitors in this endeavor – their fathers.

Whether or not this is a completely accurate description, we can certainly use the metaphor to understand the struggles children at this age experience as they attempt to control impulses and concurrently develop strict obsessive and compulsive rules. A 5-year-old's yellow vegetables can't touch the chicken on the plate, and certain things must be done in a particular order or they have to be repeated. Many age-appropriate games reinforce this rigid rule system. Kids might tell each other, "If you step on a crack, you get eaten by a crocodile. If you fall off the line, you get eaten by a lion."

In life, most transitions begin with the establishment of a very orderly structure, which gives one a feeling of security as the world changes. With further development, the evolving human is able to adapt some of these rules to different situations. Children who can't move past this phase of very strict rules and order may struggle with the day-to-day inconsistencies of life or suffer from obsessive-compulsive disorder. Remember, though, that at 4 to 6 years of age, such behavior is the norm. This process is essential to learning to deal with reality as the child navigates between desires and drives and the acceptable standards of society.

School becomes the primary stage for these developmental advances. In class, children are expected to sit still for long periods of time, to follow directions and to complete tasks. They are encouraged to work together, and they are forced to delay gratification and to restrain themselves in order to meet expected standards of behavior. The development of these social skills prepares children to navigate group environments far into the future.

A Tricky Discipline: The Importance of Setting and Enforcing Limits

Occasionally, at a checkup I'll ask a child: "How was your summer vacation? What did you do?"

Often the answer is, "Nothing."

Then, the child's parent will stare at him with a look of disbelief and ask, "What do you mean nothing? Didn't we go to Disneyworld?"

But for the child, such trips may be the norm and subconsciously what he or she has come to expect, as something similar happens every vacation. You'd probably have to shoot some of these kids into outer space before they'd offer a more excited answer.

As we raise children, most of us reflect on our own childhoods. We live in the present but we carry the past along with us. For better or worse, watching the way your child experiences the world rekindles experiences you yourself had while going through the same processes. A mom may feel sadness because she was deprived in her childhood of a pleasure her child is now enjoying. Another may delight in fond memories of similar events. Some parents who felt they were deprived as children resent the benefits that their own children have. People who were raised in a lower economic tier may feel their children are spoiled. Others may wish to bestow the things they wanted and couldn't have upon their children. That doesn't mean you have to buy your child a BMW as soon as he gets his driver's license. You can give children chores along with an appropriate allowance. They can save this money for future purposes, which will teach them responsibility.

We try not to make the same mistakes as our parents did, only to end up making our own brand-new mistakes. Parents may have felt overindulged or smothered or ignored as children. These feelings will affect the way they raise their progeny. Still, everything is relative. If you grew up in poverty and you are now living in a more affluent community, it is not necessarily correct to intentionally deprive your child in order not to "spoil" them. On the other hand, doing the right thing for a child doesn't always mean doing what the child wants, and your children may not always be happy with you as a result. Remember: You are their parent, not their friend. This can be a difficult concept to master. The Polish pediatrician, writer, educator and early 20th century child advocate Janusz Korchak, MD, wrote about this issue in his seminal book *How to Love a Child*, which has been translated into many languages, but not into English.

Korchak asks whether loving your child means allowing anything and everything. His answer: Not on your life. By prohibiting things, Korchak explains, a parent coaxes the will in the direction of self-control and self-denial. This approach also encourages inventiveness, he says, by enabling a child to operate within a limited sphere. What limits the sphere? Those all-important societal expectations.

In an opinion piece for the *New York Times*, Op-Ed Columnist Frank Bruni (who is childless) shared a few observations on parenting. He stated: "Parents routinely surrender control when they shouldn't, replacing rules with requests, and children are expected to chart their own routes to good behavior, using the faulty GPS' of their flowering consciences, I suppose. Families are run as democracies."

A lax disciplinary approach in childhood can work out to the detriment of a child as he grows older and struggles to manage his own behavior. "Sidney" was a socially awkward teenage patient of mine who had a tendency toward extreme moodiness and rapid mood swings. After reviewing the results of one of his examinations, I mentioned to Sidney that he was too heavy. I emphasized that my concern was for his health and that his being overweight was a risk factor for future medical conditions. As we discussed the behaviors that were contributing to this problem, it came to light that Sidney spent six hours a day on some sort of screen. We discussed the negative implications of this excessive time commitment, both relating to the weight issue and to his sense of social isolation. Sidney vehemently defended the value of this activity. I could see mom starting to twitch as I discussed the importance of replacing the time spent in the virtual world with physical activity and interpersonal relationships. I remain skeptical about her ability to implement this intervention.

We want our children to love us, and one of the hardest parts of being a parent is seeing your child in pain, be it physical or emotional. It's natural for a parent to try to minimize that pain, but in the process of trying to avoid our child's tears and pouts, we're sometimes blackmailed into responses that aren't in the best interest of the child over the long term.

Physicians certainly aren't immune to the tensions of parenthood. When an old friend, psychiatrist Jane Hatheway, MD, was asked to describe parenthood to a group of medical residents, she described being a parent as the most humbling experience possible. It's also the hardest job in the world, and parents often have to wait 20 or more years to see how things turn out.

In our times, when the concept of immediate gratification is increasingly prevalent, it seems to have become more important to make a child happy than to allow him to deal with frustration and disappointment. As a result, children don't gain the coping tools they need to thrive later on in life.

In the 1990s, the practice of "back to sleep" came into favor, with newborns being encouraged to sleep on their backs to reduce the incidence of SIDS (sudden infant death syndrome). Soon, we in the medical field noticed a lot of babies developing flat heads (called "plagiocephaly"). In addition, motor development was somewhat slower, with babies rolling over later and sitting up at an older age.

In response, pediatricians started encouraging "tummy time," periods during which babies were laid on their stomachs to take pressure off the backs of their heads. Babies would often get frustrated on their tummies, and in response some parents would immediately roll them onto their backs. I'd tell these parents that a little frustration is not a bad thing. Complacence can result in inertia, while frustration can motivate. Or as

Thomas Edison once said, "Discontent is the first necessity of progress." When a baby is on her stomach, she strengthens the neck and tries to roll over. This does not mean, of course, that we want to constantly frustrate our children. Everything in moderation.

An old medical anecdote recalls the tale of a mother who brought her son, Johnny, to the psychiatrist with the complaint that he wouldn't listen to her. The psychiatrist asked the mother to give him an example.

"I had to ask him to take out the garbage 20 times before he finally did it," the mother said.

The psychiatrist listened and then asked her why she thought he'd finally performed the task after ignoring her request 19 times previously.

The mom responded, "I guess he knew at that point I really meant it."

Most children truly do want to please their parents. Conflict arises, though, when satisfying a parent interferes with the child's desire for pleasure. Part of becoming a responsible adult is learning to at times put aside one's immediate satisfaction to achieve a higher goal or to simply please someone you care about. Parents need to demonstrate this skill to their progeny both in actions and words.

Another reason why children misbehave? They feel ignored and decide that a bit of notoriety is better than no attention at all. Kids are sure to act out if they discover that doing so is the most effective way to gain a parent's consideration. That may include behaving poorly or even playing sick. Of all the advice I as a pediatrician can give to new and prospective parents, the most important piece is that you should always make your children feel loved – for who they are; not for who you want them to be. The next best piece of advice I can give is that parents should set reasonable limits on acceptable behavior. It is even more important to be a good role model for your children. How you behave in your day-to-day life sets the structure for what your children will come to consider the norm. It doesn't mean much for you to tell your child to play fair and to be a good sport if, as coach of the team, your only goal is to win at all costs. When I was coaching a number of youth teams in my town, some fellow parent coaches would only play their best players in order to win, while the other less-talented team members sat on the bench observing the action. Some of these parents would even try to intimidate the adolescent umpires or referees in order to push more of the judgments in their favor. What kind of lesson do you think this teaches the children? It is well known that it is more important for children to play than for them to win. For a child, being forced to sit on the bench and watch while the other players win is very discouraging. By treating other people fairly and with respect, a parent teaches his or her child that this is the acceptable way to treat other human beings and even animals. The child who gets kicked by his parents ends up kicking the dog, and children who are abused when they are young are more likely to become abusive parents themselves.

What truly determines how a child will turn out? The end result is a combination of both nature and nurture. A supportive environment helps a child achieve his or her full potential, which is in turn determined by physical and mental abilities as well as temperament. Studies have shown that children display different temperaments beginning immediately after birth, even before they've left the nursery. An interesting new area of research called "epigenetics" even proposes that environmental factors can change genetics by turning certain genes on and off. So is it nature or nurture that matters more? The two camps of this age-old debate continue to argue.

From Chattel to Little Caesar: The Child's Changing Status

"Max" was an 18-month-old patient of mine who was slightly delayed in his motor development and was only just beginning to walk. His parents were very concerned. I listened to their concerns and examined him carefully. Everything was normal except for his muscle tone, which was low. They asked me about the implications of this hypotonia. I tried to reassure them about his bright prospects, making only the proviso that he would probably not become an Olympic athlete. A glum silence fell over the room. Max's parents were so upset by my statement that they soon scheduled a consultation with a pediatric neurologist. The neurologist corroborated my opinion, but he made no mention of the Olympics. Max is now in his 20s. He attends college, but as of yet, he hasn't tried out for international athletic competition.

Historically, children were considered chattel. Mothers usually had many children and they often died early themselves in childbirth. The children were there to help with work around the farm, and the saying that "children should be seen and not heard" gained popularity in common parlance. As society became industrialized and parents were better able to control the size of their families, children gained more value. In the mid-20th century, the pendulum completed its swing in the opposite direction, and parents became the root of all of their children's problems. Freud popularized the belief that we are all products of our upbringing, with our mothers playing a crucial role in how we eventually turn out. Even now, mothers often take the blame for all of their children's failures. (Unfortunately, they do not also receive credit for any successes those offspring enjoy.)

In these enlightened times, children have become, for most parents, the center of the universe. Many parents have resultantly become hostage to the whims and wants of their Messianic progeny, and now base their sense of success on their child's happiness and accomplishments. Conversely, if the child is unhappy, they have failed. If these parents' offspring are not at the top in their class academically, athletically and socially, the parents feel they haven't done their jobs. Every possible attempt is made to allow the child to reach his or her predetermined potential for excellence.

A snarky joke heard around my parts asks, "What is the definition of a genius?" The answer: "Being a 'C' student in Bergen County, New Jersey," although the joke is applicable to any success-driven and somewhat affluent community.

Laughter and Other Life Skills: The 5-Year Checkup and beyond

"Evan" was sitting on my examination table in his underwear with a big smile on his face. Evan had been a high-risk baby. After birth, we'd been concerned about his poor feeding and muscle tone, his nystagmus (rapid horizontal eye movements) and his big head. There was also concern that Evan was blind, although my gut feeling was that he could see and would be fine. So now here he was, sitting on the examination table at age 5 with none of the aforementioned problems, except perhaps the big head. As I usually do, I started conversing with Evan about his day, his interests and his likes and his dislikes. (I enjoy teasing the kids that I know well, as it often puts them at ease.) Evan was looking at me and smiling and for some reason, I decided to ask him if he knew any jokes.

Without hesitation, Evan responded: "Why did Tigger stick his head down the toilet?"

After a pause, I answered: "Don't know."

And with that big smile, he delivered the punchline: "He was looking for Pooh."

This was a reference to both Winnie the Pooh and actual poo (as in a bowel movement). Because of the unexpected spontaneity and the timing of this joke I began laughing hysterically, as did Evan and Evan's mom. The laughter resonated through the entire office, and I still chuckle about that checkup.

My conversation with Evan in the examination room that day illustrates several hallmarks of children in this age group: first, their ability to add context to speech and their development of a sense of humor, and second, their preoccupation with excretory functions. The 5-Year Checkup is one of the most intense in the pediatric repertoire. Aside from taking the usual history and doing the physical exam, your child will also have a blood test for anemia and cholesterol, vision and hearing screenings and extensive developmental screening questions, followed by the required kindergarten immunizations. In addition, after the exam I ask children to draw some shapes and write their names.

During that checkup, Evan had been intrigued by my bowtie, so at a later office visit I gave him a bowtie that one of my sons wore when he was little. I recently saw Evan for his 6-Year Checkup. Evan's mom said he was concerned because he hadn't been able to think of a joke to tell me. Mom gave me a photo of Evan wearing a dress shirt and the bowtie. Despite his parents' proclivity toward casual dress, Evan now insists on wearing a bowtie to school.

Another wonderful attribute of children of this age group is their developing imaginations. Children begin creating stories while they are playing, either with dolls or with action figures. Some parents may be concerned because their child will tell them at this age about their imaginary friends, who the child may feel are quite real. The worry is that the child is telling fibs, but at this stage, this is neither unusual nor pathological.

At around age 5, most children also begin formal schooling. This requires a significant adjustment, although the change isn't as extreme as it was during my childhood. When I was growing up, kindergarten represented our first exposure to any kind of structured educational setting. Nowadays, children are introduced to this kind of orderly environment as early as 3 months of age if they attend daycare. In our area, it is unusual for a child not to be in some sort of school setting by the age of 3. How important is this? Well, in New York City and probably in other competitive cities as well, some parents have their toddlers tested and are willing to spend tens of thousands of dollars to ensure their progeny attends an *elite* nursery school. The fantasy for these parents is that enrolling their children in the proper program will set them on the path to an Ivy League college. Conversely, if their child doesn't get into the correct nursery school, their life is essentially over, and they can certainly forget Harvard! Unfortunately, at this age it is not possible to determine the ultimate intelligence of most children.

In particularly competitive regions, some parents also seek to gain an edge for their child by delaying the start of kindergarten. Theoretically, this allows the student another year to mature and fine-tune the skills she will need to excel in school. I've always questioned this logic. Do you want your child to be a little fish in a big pond or a big fish in a little pond? Recent studies indicate that this practice might actually backfire, as the older child often uses the other younger children as her role models and targets that level of achievement. This is called regression to the mean. Of course, there are individual situations in which holding a child back for specific reasons would be a good idea. A child who is very small and/ or socially or educationally immature might benefit from this strategy.

"Elizabeth" came to see me for her 8-Year Checkup. I was greeted by an adorable, cheerful and interactive girl who was doing well in the third grade and who was involved in cheerleading and gymnastics. She was dressed stylishly in an outfit she had chosen herself. She answered my questions thoroughly and she was able to willingly perform all the tasks required to complete her physical exam. Elizabeth exhibited few of the inhibitions of the younger children or the self-consciousness and angst of teenagers. Coincidentally, her mom looked relaxed and well put together. I've observed that the exhausted and careworn appearance of mothers with younger children fades at this stage. Both mother and child exhibit a more composed and self-assured view. Children are now able to attend to their own needs and so, too, once again can the parents.

After early childhood comes this relatively quiescent period, which is called "latency." Latency covers the time between when a child has settled into school up until the onset of puberty. By this point, most children have adapted to the rules of school, home and society. They start to develop closer friendships. For the most part, they have gained control over their impulses. Freud would say that children in this phase have resolved their Oedipal complexes. In problem cases, some of the skills necessary for advancing to the next stage of development haven't been mastered yet, but barring emotional or situational problems, this is a relatively untroubled period.

By latency, most children have adjusted to the routines of life. They start engaging in extracurricular activities such as organized sports, religion classes, hobbies, social groups or music lessons. They learn to work in an integrated fashion as a member of a team, and they learn to temporarily put aside their own needs to further the betterment of the group, which is a basic concept essential to a healthy adulthood. Part of this process includes conceptualizing the notion that not everything is a result of a child's thought or action: *I may want something, but it may not be available.* Or: *I might do something and the result is not what I thought it would be.* The child learns to repress some of his or her more primitive thoughts, although the remnants of them exist even into adulthood. (Just think about the sports fan who wears his hat cocked at a certain angle in order to ensure a win, or the one who is convinced his team lost just because he stopped watching the game.) It is essential for a child to abandon the fantasy of having control over the universe if he or she is to learn how to compromise, and conciliation is essential to developing healthy relationships.

Stomachaches and Other Common Ailments: Should You Worry?

Recently, 11-and-a-half-year-old "Jessie" was brought to me by her father. She had a sudden onset of severe abdominal pain and vomiting for several hours after going on a school trip on a hot summer day. She had only eaten a red slushy for lunch, and she'd been fine up till that point. Her father was very concerned because he'd had a ruptured appendix at 12. Fortunately, the history and physical exam pointed away from a surgical condition. I sent her home on clear fluids and warned them about the signs that would make me concerned. Dad was told to call me if she was not improving. She recovered just fine.

One of the most common complaints pediatricians treat school-aged children for is stomachache. The differential diagnosis (the potential causes) can be mind-boggling. One of the most common parental concerns is acute appendicitis. The book *Cope's Early Diagnosis of the Acute Abdomen* by Zachary Cope, MD, has been, for me, an instrumental resource for concisely determining the pertinent history and clinical findings associated with surgical conditions relating to acute abdominal pain.

Abdominal pain is commonly caused by constipation or gastroenteritis (stomach viruses). Some children might have lactose intolerance, which is less common in those of Northern European descent. These patients can't digest milk sugar, which results in abdominal pain, bloating and diarrhea. This is treatable by reducing or eliminating milk sugar. Other less likely causes are inflammatory bowel disease and other immunological conditions, gynecological or urinary issues, infection, reactions to foods, drugs or poisons, and less frequently, abnormalities in the body's biological pathways, anatomic issues or tumors. The most common kind of abdominal pain is called functional abdominal pain. When I was chairman of the department of pediatrics at The Valley Hospital in Ridgewood, New Jersey, I enjoyed the perk of being interviewed by CBS New York

Reporter Pat Farnack about abdominal pain in children. She interviewed me for 45 minutes and distilled our entire interview into a one-minute slot. A lot was left out, but she captured the most salient points.

Put simply, tummy aches in children are like headaches in adults. In fact, many children who have tummy aches go on to develop headaches as they get older. For the most part, children with recurrent abdominal pain who are otherwise healthy – which is to say, growing well with good appetite and no fever, vomiting, diarrhea or constipation – tend not to have a serious underlying problem.

Why do so many otherwise healthy children suffer from abdominal pain with no obvious cause? Are they faking? Most of the time they are not. It is a rare case in which a child consciously fakes an illness for some psychological or physical gain, otherwise known as malingering. Children often malinger to get extra attention from their parents or to avoid an activity in which they don't want to participate. Most cases are stress-related, and the pain is real. It can be sensed by the child as a tightness or fullness in the belly similar to the tightness around the entire head that many adults feel when they are stressed. They are not emotionally equipped to understand the connection, and often their parents haven't made the connection either. Some parents had similar symptoms when they were children, and they may even continue to suffer from them as adults. When a pediatrician can get a parent to see the connection between stress, headache and stomachache, a comforting light bulb often goes on in the parent's head that allows him or her to view the situation in a less threatening light.

When I was in fifth grade, I had a horrible, mean teacher, Miss McLean. She was constantly screaming at the students. If tummy aches in children are like headaches in adults, I guess my reaction to her was a bit precocious: I would walk home for lunch almost daily with a headache and refuse to go back to school in the afternoon. I give my mother credit for listening to me, as I had always enjoyed school. She contacted several of my classmates' parents to discuss the situation. All the parents received the same evaluation of this teacher from their children. My headaches disappeared, along with Miss McLean, who took an early retirement. I wasn't faking it, and I haven't had any major problems with headaches since.

It is important to consider the circumstances occurring around the time of a child's pain. Is it every morning except on weekends and holidays? In that case, it may be related to school issues. Is it each Sunday night prior to the start of the school week? The child might be nervously anticipating a separation from the parents. Sometimes stomachaches are associated with family problems, either emotional or health-related. Some children suffer before bedtime due to fear of nightmares. Again, a careful history and physical examination is the key to a correct diagnosis.

When evaluating the child, parents and pediatrician must consider the patterns exhibited by the child. Does the child frequently complain or is complaining a rare occurrence? If complaining is rare, the problem deserves a bit of attention and consideration. Is the child diligent about school or happy to miss a day? Sometimes, too, a kid just needs a break. I call it a "Mental Health Day," and its effect is comparable to recharging a car's run-down battery. This mental time out may give the student a little time off from the demands of school and possibly other activities. A slight break in the routine can be amazingly reinvigorating.

Severe abdominal pain is another matter, and it can have different causes. An article in the June 2013 issue of *Pediatrics* reviewed 10,000 cases of children who presented to the emergency room at the University of Pittsburgh Medical Center with abdominal pain. The study found that a full 25 percent of the cases were a result of constipation. The parents are usually not aware that this is the cause; they only see their children writhing in pain. I have even encountered situations in which these constipated children manifest a symptom called paradoxical diarrhea. The child has liquid stool, and often soils his underwear because any solid excrement is blocked from elimination by the impacted feces further down the colon. The parents bring their children to the office because of the symptom of diarrhea, when in fact the treatment needs to be directed toward the real problem: the constipation.

I emphasize to my colleagues that they should always check for constipation before sending a child to the hospital for abdominal pain, and my advice is the same for parents. Don't be afraid to roll up your sleeves and get your hands dirty! A rectal examination could help you to avoid a costly and traumatic visit to the ER.

Early in my career, a mom brought her 4-year-old child to the office for belly pain. While I was examining the patient, I felt a large mass in his lower abdomen. Having recently finished my residency, I was convinced that the child had a tumor. I consulted with my senior partner, Donald Wolmer, MD, who asked me if I had done a rectal exam. I had not. I performed the rectal examination and discovered that the child was backed up with stool. The treatment required was an enema rather than surgery. As a pediatrician, I have no reservations against examining the body's excrement in order to make a correct diagnosis. I encourage parents to follow my lead.

Obesity and Its Causes: Managing Your Child's Weight and Health

"Dawn," a 10-year-old female patient of mine, was becoming progressively more overweight. At four feet, eight inches tall, she weighed 160 pounds and struggled even to climb onto the examination table. During our initial meeting, I had noticed her struggling to breathe as we sat and talked. Dawn had Pickwickian Syndrome. This condition, named for an obese character in a Charles Dickens novel, can lead to reduced oxygen in the blood and strain on the heart in addition to sleep apnea. I had previously counseled Dawn's mother, who was overweight herself, about the problem.

When Dawn reached 160 pounds, I told her mother point-blank that unless the girl made changes to her lifestyle, she would die. Dawn became involved in a weight-loss program and started dropping pounds. With much work and much encouragement, she'd soon lost 40 pounds. One year later, she'd gained back all of the weight and then some. Her involvement and interest in the weight-loss endeavor diminished, as did our relationship. I am sure both Dawn and her mother felt not only that they'd failed in their mission, but also that they'd disappointed me.

Obesity is a major health issue facing the current generation of kids, and it is no less than an epidemic. At this point, up to 40 percent of our children are either overweight or obese. But obesity itself is just part of the problem. Being overweight leads to many additional health issues, including an increased incidence of diabetes, high blood pressure and hyperlipidemia (an increase in cholesterol and other unhealthy fats). It also elevates the risk of heart disease and even fatty inflammation of the liver. It additionally can result in early puberty in girls, menstrual and other hormonal abnormalities, and an increased risk for certain types of cancer.

Parents must also consider the effect obesity has on the self-esteem of a child. Our cultural standard for physical attractiveness in modern times has been the size-two model or actress, and the plump, Renoir-style beauty of eras passed is no longer in vogue. It is not surprising that overweight girls are particularly affected by poor self-images, but boys may be affected, too, especially when their weight interferes with their athletic performance.

What causes obesity? The answer is multifactorial, but let's start with a basic law of physics: You cannot simply create matter. You can only add or take away existing matter. In order to gain weight, you must consume more calories than you expend. (This excludes certain rare, serious conditions in which a child might retain fluid, such as heart or kidney failure.) Both the amount and kinds of food you ingest play an important role in this process. Not all foods are created equally. As chefs love to remind us, fat is flavor. It also has more than twice as many calories per portion as any other food type. Fried foods are more calorically intense than the same food baked or broiled. So sad!

What's to be done? So far, science has been stumped. Years ago, food scientists created a non-absorbable kind of fat called "Olestra." In theory, this meant that you could have your cake and eat it, too. Unfortunately, the majority of the people who ate food prepared with Olestra became extremely flatulent or developed diarrhea. So perhaps there is no easy fix.

Certain kinds of foods, like proteins, require that the body use more calories to digest them, which lessens their caloric impact. Complex carbohydrates, which are usually present in fruit, vegetables and whole grains, release their sugars more evenly than simple sugars or processed grains. Consuming these simple and processed foods results in sugar spikes, which create new hunger pangs in a person soon after he or she has eaten.

Often, parents overestimate how much food a child needs to eat to maintain proper health. There are many guides for determining the proper portion sizes for your child, but the sizes of the portions they are served in restaurants aren't one of them. In the documentary film *Supersize Me*, director Morgan Spurlock documented the detrimental effects of both fast foods and large portion sizes. For a month, Spurlock ate at McDonalds three meals a day and never refused "supersized" portions when they were offered to him. By the end of his experiment, he'd gained 25 pounds and was suffering from liver inflammation and depression. Over the years, individual portions sizes have increased exponentially. A typical serving of soda, which was once seven ounces, is now a liter, and there has been a correspondingly large increase in the size of a serving of French fries. Former New York City Mayor Michael Bloomberg recently tried to address the soda issue by limiting the sale of oversized beverages. The public was not happy, and the action is being contested in court.

Historically, skinny kids were considered to be sickly. I myself was a relatively skinny kid until about 4 years of age. My parents were likely concerned that I was ill because I wasn't plump enough, and the medical wisdom of the times dictated that the tonsils were unnecessary structures that ought to be removed at the slightest provocation, so I was scheduled for a tonsillectomy. I was promised that I could have as much ice cream as I wanted after the procedure was finished. Thus commenced my struggle with my waistline.

Back then, plumpness was associated with well-being. This distorted concept still exists today, although it is more prevalent in certain cultures than in others, and it contributes to the epidemic of obesity. "Lean and mean," on the other hand, is a common term use to describe a fit, toned body. As a matter of fact, because 40 percent of children are now overweight, our views of who is skinny and who is fat have become distorted. Now, most children considered "skinny" are only skinny by comparison. In actuality, they are at healthy weights based on the scientific tables.

In former times, affluence was associated with corpulence. In the United States today, poverty contributes to the obesity problem, as fast food is more readily available than fresh fruit and vegetables in impoverished areas. There has recently been a slight decrease in obesity in impoverished children, which may be due to some of the federal programs that have put healthy meals in schools.

The next piece of the childhood obesity puzzle is the sedentary lifestyle prevalent in much of modern American society. Again, many factors contribute to the issue. When I was a youngster, if we wanted to play, we'd knock on our friends' doors and invite them out to play in the street or on the playground. Being kidnapped or getting run over by a driver who was high on drugs or busy texting wasn't a concern. We rode our bikes everywhere without serious worry. The times have changed. Most families now have two working parents. Most kids' activities now need to be organized and supervised, and children are left at home unsupervised with little to do until their parents return from work.

Misconceptions about exercise also contribute to obesity. I often encounter patients who are confused because they are overweight despite the fact that they are quite active. Exercise is not the panacea. Unless you are an Olympic swimmer or a marathon runner, you simply cannot burn off the calories you ingest through excessive eating. The average person burns, at most, 400 to 500 calories per hour by jogging, which can be easily undone by eating just a slice of pizza or a few cookies. But exercise has additional benefits. For one, if a child is exercising he is usually not eating. Exercise also helps maintain weight as well as increasing the body's sensitivity to insulin. That increased responsiveness to insulin decreases the likelihood of diabetes and improves the efficiency of heart contractions. In addition, strenuous exercise releases endorphins, which are brain chemicals that decrease anxiety and improve a person's mood. So not only is exercise good for you and your kids, it actually, chemically, makes you feel good.

Obesity is also closely connected to what I call "screen time," or time spent in front of any kind of screen. This includes, television, video games, computers, tablets, and smartphones. Each of these devices reduces time spent exercising, but excessive screen time presents additional dangers. One concern is eye-strain, which occurs when eye muscles are overused as a child or adult works to react to the rapid visual changes on a screen. This isn't a permanent issue, although I am convinced that more children will need spectacles because of its long-term effects. Recently I saw an older teenager for his checkup. His only complaints were some neck and back pain. When I asked him about possible causes, he admitted to spending five to six hours daily on the screen. "Text thumbs" and carpal tunnel syndrome resulting from repetitive use of certain muscle groups have been identified as just a few of the various physical problems that can arise from excessive use of these devices. I am additionally convinced that we will see a higher incidence of neck and back disease related to excessive use of computer screens due to the back and neck positioning these devices require.

Video games can also be addictive, and the constant stimulation of these games makes ordinary life seem dull by comparison. One recent study in a 2012 issue of the *Journal of Behavioral Addictions* suggested that even cell phone use can be addicting, as it stimulates the part of the brain associated with rewards. Why do we have to check our cell phones instantaneously each time a text message or e-mail comes in? How often is it that important?

Prolonged time in the virtual world can also lead to social isolation. Studies have shown that prolonged time on the screen leads to an increased incidence of depression. The verdict is not in as to whether exposure to violent video games leads to an increased level of violence, but evidence shows that people consume 25 percent more food while watching television than they would otherwise. On top of this, 50 percent of television commercials are food-related, and we're not talking about fruit- and vegetable-related. In a 2012 cataloguing of food advertising by the Center for Science in the Public Interest, 69 percent of food-related commercials on the popular children's network *Nickelodeon* were categorized as advertising foods of poor nutritional value that either had added sugar or were fast foods.

In the end, there are no quick fixes to the problem of obesity in children and adults. Diets just don't work. If there were a diet that truly worked, there wouldn't be hundreds of new diet books written each year. Diets have led to more weight lost and then regained than can ever be counted. The real treatment for obesity is long-term lifestyle changes, and the best results occur when your entire family is involved in the change.

One major difference between children and adults is that children not only grow out but also up. The only way adults grow is out, and they must also contend with the dreaded "decade creep," or the five extra pounds per decade that seem to magically appear each decade after age 20. In most children who are overweight but not obese, weight loss isn't essential. What is crucial is slowing the weight gain down to allow the growth to catch up.

Each One Special: Understanding Ability and Disability

I recently had a consult with a young Indian couple who was concerned about their 2-and-a-half-year-old boy. The mom was an occupational therapist who helped patients to develop fine-motor coordination in day-to-day activities, and she was worried because "Krish" wasn't able to recognize his letters and because he became frustrated quickly when she tried to get him to copy. My interaction with Krish revealed him to be an adorable, appropriately interactive little boy who was performing his milestones without a problem. I even checked his pencil grip, which was more correct than mine. I reassured mom and dad that their son was acting appropriately in all aspects.

Despite parents' unreasonable hopes and expectations, it is rare that a little boy of this age will be able to sit and perform a task for more than a few minutes at a time. Physical play is a different story.

To reiterate, young boys are emotionally rather un-evolved when compared to girls. It's not unusual to see a little girl sitting quietly and pasting or coloring while her male counterparts struggle to focus and concentrate. Girls are simply better adapted in the early grades to sit, concentrate and learn. This puts boys at a disadvantage, as their inability to sit still means they are often less favored by many teachers. Rest assured that the skill can and does develop, usually by the third or fourth grade.

Until recently, the concepts of "smart" and "stupid" prevailed in school, as in: You were either smart or you were stupid and that was that. Early on, teachers segregated students by placing the "smartest" of the students in a higher-achieving class. In a way, this created a self-fulfilling prophecy, as higher achievers were exposed to the most challenging material and the most intense competition and so progressed faster. At a certain point on his journey through the system, the "slower" child would become stuck in his assigned level as the separation of classes widened and it became more difficult to change or improve. This concept of "smart or stupid" was, of course, a gross oversimplification, and the labels were often incorrect anyway. For the most part, you were considered smart if you did well in most or all subjects. However, there are people who do quite well in only a few subjects. If these people make it through to higher education and begin to focus on their areas of skill and interest, they can excel. The most extreme examples of this are children with high-functioning Asperger's syndrome. They can excel in arcane areas of knowledge and yet they have no concept of emotional content. They don't pick up on humor and have a tough time with social skills and with forming relationships with other human beings. Some of the most revolutionary figures in science probably had a form of this syndrome. Albert Einstein comes to mind: always disheveled, going outdoors in his pajamas with one shoe on and one shoe off. He supposedly didn't speak until he was 4 years old. Although he wasn't communicating verbally, his mind developed an incredible ability to see things spatially. This ability allowed him to view previously baffling problems in a unique way, and he was able to propose novel theories that led to solutions to these enigmas. Better not to underestimate a "slow child."

Concern about ADHD (attention deficit hyperactivity disorder) is one of the most common neurological and behavioral issues that pediatricians encounter. In this disorder, a child has deficiencies in focusing and possibly other personality traits, and he or she is often hyperactive, impulsive and fidgety. The problem is best understood as a deficiency in the part of the brain that filters out extraneous stimuli. To help parents grasp how ADHD affects a child, I ask them to think about a situation in which they're trying to concentrate on a difficult problem as a noisy truck drives by, or a clock ticks loudly, or a chair squeaks repeatedly, and their focus gravitates irresistibly toward those noises rather than staying on the task at hand.

There is no specific test that identifies this condition, because it is what is known as a "symptom complex," not a disease, and it can have different causes. Other medical or behavioral conditions may also mimic ADHD. ADHD is estimated to occur in five to 10 percent of children, and it's becoming even more prevalent in our society as physical work is continually supplanted by more academic and technically oriented occupations, which require greater concentration. Students with ADHD may have a high IQ, but they can't finish tasks because they're unable to stay focused and are easily distracted. If the disorder is left untreated, either behaviorally or medically, these children can become school failures.

The best way for a pediatrician to diagnose ADHD is by taking a careful history of the child, including reviewing his or her school reports and performing a physical examination that eliminates other physical causes for the behavior constellation. The former designation of this symptom complex was ADD, with or without hyperactivity. ADHD is a term that encompasses both situations. Children with hyperactivity are easier to diagnose because their inability to sit still is conspicuously disruptive in class. Girls tend to display hyperactivity less frequently. Children of higher intelligence who don't display hyperactivity can slip through the cracks until the later grades when the work gets more complicated and their difficulty focusing overrides their innate intelligence.

Back in the late 1960s and early 1970s, Ben F. Feingold, MD, proposed that salicylates both naturally present in certain foods and artificially included in food additives, artificial coloring, flavoring and sweeteners played a role in the symptoms of ADHD. By carefully eliminating all of these items from a child's diet, the thinking went, you could improve or eliminate the symptoms. Unfortunately, sticking to such a regimen was very complicated and time-consuming because salicylates are ubiquitous in the average diet. Subsequent studies have shown that such dietary changes have little or no effect on behavior, and that the time spent trying to eliminate these foods might have been better spent dealing directly with the child's behavioral and educational issues. Additional concerns about the relationship between sweets or other food items and worsening symptoms have been proposed but remain unsubstantiated. What I suggest to parents is that if their child consistently reacts poorly to a particular food, they should avoid it.

So how can a parent best support a child struggling with focus and behavior? The first step is to accept the problem: The ADHD and all its possible associated symptoms. The next step is to realize that the child is not intentionally behaving in an unruly fashion. Finally, parents should give the child whatever support he needs. This support may come in the form of extra time or help in school, psychological encouragement to help the child navigate difficulties arising with school and personal relationships, or medication if necessary.

I often tell parents who come to me to discuss concerns about ADHD that 20 years ago, I would've had to spend half an hour convincing them why they needed to medicate their child. Today, I have to spend the same amount of time convincing them that their child *doesn't* need medication.

Ultimately, learning is unique to each individual. Some people are better visual learners and learn best by watching for cues. Others learn more effectively by listening. I've discovered that I learn best by listening and then writing. This adds a tactile component to the learning process. For children with specific learning disabilities, multiple modalities are sometimes required to get the lesson into the brain.

Some children with specific learning disabilities have a difficult time deciphering written language or oral communication. These students need to be identified and taught to their strengths. For instance, a poor visual learner might need to have all of her lessons recorded, while a child who has a focusing issue might need to be put in a smaller class, given more time for tests and possibly take medication. A child with dysgraphia, or an inability to write, needs occupational therapy to strengthen and coordinate the hand muscles, plus perhaps earlier exposure to keyboards and less emphasis on handwriting tasks. A slap on the hand with a ruler for sloppy penmanship will not help this child. (It appears that many physicians suffer from a form of dysgraphia. Just look at the penmanship on most prescriptions! Thank goodness we are moving toward electronic prescribing.)

When I was a pediatric resident, I took an elective in learning disabilities at New York University with two of the most renowned experts of the time, psychologists Rosa Hagin and Archie A. Silver M.D. One of the projects they were working on at the time involved screening students in a public school kindergarten class for potential learning disabilities, and we residents helped by observing specific skills. One of the skills we watched for was the child's awareness of where her fingers were. A deficiency in this area was called "finger agnosia." Another task involved pencil grip. Under supervision, I was to evaluate the children, but I discovered that I was unable to evaluate this particular task properly, as I'd been holding my pencil incorrectly all my life.

I never thought about how I learned best until I took that elective with Drs. Hagin and Silver. Some of my medical student classmates were able to pick up a textbook and read it from cover to cover. This never worked for me. I became bored and distracted. But if I came across an interesting case, I'd read everything I could find about it. I took in new knowledge best when I had a ready application for it.

When I perform a yearly checkup, another important area I explore that may influence learning is the child's social history. This involves getting up to speed on the child's living arrangements, which can vary greatly from family to family, as discussed earlier. Some children struggle in school due to physical or emotional issues such as being malnourished or neglected, anxious or depressed. Anxiety can make concentrating difficult, while depression can cause a decrease in energy or a loss of motivation. Feeling unwell due either to illness or malnutrition affects both energy levels and the ability to concentrate.

Most people have heard of IQ (intellectual quotient), but it's important to be aware of a lesser-known and equally important concept called EQ (emotional quotient.) EQ is a quality that can also be understood as "people smarts." People who have this kind of intelligence are able to read others and to understand their emotions, motivations, strengths and weaknesses. They can then use this knowledge to achieve their desired goals. People with this skill set excel in sales and positions that require interpersonal skills. The top managers in business and government must have both EQ and IQ. These people may or may not have excelled in school. Children on the autism spectrum, specifically those with Asperger's syndrome, lack EQ but can develop specific areas of expertise even as they continue to struggle with deficits in many other areas. So much for the simple concepts of smart and stupid!

Each One Different: Nurturing Your Child's Individuality

Not every child is a genius or enjoys perfect health, but every child is certainly special, and each child is undeniably different. "Samuel" was born more than 25 years ago, 10 weeks early, to an older, first-time mother. At the time, we pediatricians were called to all difficult or premature deliveries. After learning that Samuel's mother was in labor, I rushed from my office to the delivery room, where I would normally change into my scrub suit. I was met at the door by a delivery room nurse and was instead rushed to the delivery room in my street clothes.

The baby had just been delivered, blue and with no heart rate. I began resuscitative efforts, establishing an airway, then breathing and trying to get his heart to start beating. Within ten minutes, Samuel had a heart rate and was ventilated. The regional neonatal intensive care unit had been called and was on its way. Until they arrived with their more advanced life support, we had to keep Samuel stable. The first days of Samuel's life ran a very stormy course, and he was in the NICU for a prolonged period.

Samuel survived, much to his parents' delight, but he was significantly impaired. Samuel had severe cerebral palsy, a condition resulting in muscle tightness that made it hard for him to get around and for others to understand his speech. Samuel was blessed with a sunny disposition, an excellent memory and loving parents. Several years later, his parents had a healthy, beautiful little girl. Today, Samuel gets around on his own, although with age this is becoming more difficult. He attends special programs and works painstakingly to make himself understood. But he lights up every room he enters with his smile and his bubbly personality. He is one of a number of my patients, both healthy and disabled, who brighten my day each time I encounter them in the office.

Parents often compare one of their children to another and this is rarely helpful. Temperament, birth order and changing family situations all play a role in a child's ultimate character. One of my children is a night owl; the other is not. One lives to eat, while the other eats to live. My first-born sees things in very concrete terms, while my next is artistic. I jokingly tell my patients that if I threw my two kids in the blender and combined all of their unique traits, they would make one perfect child. Here's to difference!

Vulnerable Child, Vulnerable Family: Understanding the Toll of Illness

"Donald," an only child, suffered an episode of bronchiolitis (wheezing following an upper respiratory infection) when he was an infant. Each time he had a cold and cough after this, Donald's mom would become convinced he was wheezing and bring him in to see the doctor. One year, Donald was seen 50 times in our office. His mother also brought him to a lung specialist, or pulmonologist.

For many years we worked in conjunction with this pulmonologist, even once calling child protective services in an attempt to try to minimize the toll these perceived catastrophes were taking on Donald. Over time, we were able to gradually alter his mother's perception of her son's well-being. Through careful phone screening, we monitored the number of sick visits and severely limited the number of times we allowed her to bring him to the office. However, this took an incredible amount of time and effort. We even threatened to dismiss Donald's mother from our practice if she didn't reduce her office visits. At one point, I told the mom, point blank: "If you don't trust my medical judgment after all these years, you need to find another pediatrician."

By then, we had developed a caring relationship with both Donald and his mother, so the strategy worked. Today, Donald is a healthy teenager with mild allergy symptoms who is no longer treated for asthma with the onset of each cold and cough. His mother even allowed him to go abroad with his class for two weeks, although not before he obtained a medical clearance prior to the trip. He survived and returned home with a newfound enthusiasm.

A child's illness can take a toll on the family that lasts far into the future. Sometimes, as in Donald's case, a child who has a perceived serious illness recovers but continues to be treated by one or both parents as if he is still chronically sick. This is called the "vulnerable child condition," and it is similar in many ways to post-traumatic stress disorder. The parents perceive each subsequent illness to be a potentially life-threatening event and react accordingly.

During my rotation through Memorial Sloan Kettering Hospital for Cancer and Allied Diseases during pediatric residency, I was regular witness to the toll of serious illness on the family unit. I saw many families who pulled together in crisis, but I encountered even more families who dissolved in the face of the stresses and sadness of a difficult illness.

"Scarlet" was born very prematurely, 14 to 15 weeks early. She was the last child born to a multiple-child family, and she had a very stormy course in her first days. Scarlet spent six weeks being intubated and mechanically ventilated and it wasn't until 6 months of age that she was able to leave the NICU. Because of her severely damaged lungs, she required multiple medications and oxygen to survive. Despite the intensive treatment and repeated courses of steroids she was given to reduce the inflammation, Scarlet was hospitalized again and again for respiratory failure. Her disease and concurrent treatment rendered her extremely swollen and immune-suppressed.

Despite the extreme unlikeliness of Scarlet's survival, her parents pushed the treatment to the max. She was transported to a major children's hospital in another city, where she remained in the hospital for four months because of her inability to sustain herself without the aid of a ventilator. The mother stayed with the baby, away from the rest of her family, until the child finally succumbed. Recently, I heard that Scarlet's parents had separated.

"Jonah" was a twin boy who developed well until 9 months of age, when his mother noticed that he seemed to be becoming less steady. Jonah was brought to a neurologist who was initially unable to pinpoint the abnormality. (It is often the mother or primary caregiver who is first to notice a problem because they are uniquely positioned to note slight changes in a child's normal activity.)

After a short while, Jonah was diagnosed definitively with glioblastoma, a type of brain tumor. His brain tumor was determined to be inoperable and the standard treatment failed. At this point, Jonah's outlook was dim and he stood little chance of survival. However, his mom persisted and became totally consumed with unrealistic hopes. The baby had two bone marrow transplants, but the tumor didn't resolve. Mom stopped working, sold her business and spent the better part of two years in the hospital with Jonah, at which point he died. Meanwhile, her other children played second fiddle. This course of events left her oldest child severely emotionally disturbed. The illness had not taken its full toll until several years afterward, when the woman and her husband divorced.

I have seen many such situations in which one or both parents' lives were consumed by a child's disability, and the illness became the center of their worlds. These parents would direct unlimited time, energy and money toward possible treatments, even if the treatments were unproven. In the meantime, all other household members became background noise. Healthy siblings were ignored and became resentful. Some brothers and sisters of handicapped or chronically ill children turn into very caring adults who enter the healing professions, but recent studies have suggested that siblings of children with disabilities have higher levels of emotional and functional impairment than children with unimpaired siblings. Parents of a sick child need to be aware of this potentiality and they must work hard to devote attention to their healthy children as well.

NINE

Adolescence

AFTER I GIVE A SHOT to one of my teenage patients, I tell the parents that if the teenager feels achy or seems out of sorts, they should administer a mild analgesic. The parents often look at me quizzically and ask, "How do I tell that?"

Point taken. Teenagers can be very moody and private creatures in the best of circumstances, and adolescence is easily the most challenging stage of childhood.

When parents complain about the difficulties they are having raising their small children, I sometimes pass on a saying: Little children, little problems. Big kids, big problems. We can think, then, of adolescents as overgrown 2-year-olds on steroids. A 2-year-old girl is trying to separate herself from her parent, upon whom she is still dependent for her daily needs, but the parent still has ultimate control. The adolescent is also trying to individuate by rebelling against her parents, but whereas the 2-year-old girl has a tricycle, the adolescent may have a car. A 2-year-old may mischievously sneak an extra piece of candy, while an adolescent may experiment with alcohol, sex or drugs. Toddlerhood and adolescence are easily the two most dangerous stages in a child's development, and each stage requires an extra dose of parental care and attention.

The Times, They Are a-Changin': Understanding the Adolescent Body

Adolescence is an all-inclusive term that includes both the physical and psychological changes that occur in a child as he or she transitions into adulthood. It is not synchronous with the term "puberty," which describes the physical and sexual maturation process. Adolescence and puberty usually coincide, but sometimes there is a lack of synchrony between them. This difference itself can cause problems, especially with early-maturing girls and late-maturing boys. Puberty is starting earlier these days – as early as 7 years of age in girls and 9 years in boys. Obesity in girls often hastens puberty, and there are concerns that certain environmental contaminants, including derivatives of plastics, might play a role in this phenomenon.

As a physical maturation process, puberty ultimately results in a sexually mature male and female, both capable of procreating. Pubertal development is medically broken down into either five or six stages, which are called the Tanner Stages. The pre-pubertal stage is known as Tanner One, and puberty eventually ends with Tanner Stage Five or Six, depending on the designation. There is usually a specific order of development and growth that occurs in between, with menstruation often starting at stage Three or Four in girls and the maximum growth spurts occurring around Tanner Stage Four in boys. Of course, there are exceptions. Occasionally a girl will have her period soon after breast development or a boy will stop growing before he is fully sexually mature. The period of maximal growth usually lasts three to four years, and girls usually stop growing within two years of their first periods.

In girls, the process often begins with breast development, although a former mentor of mine, Edward Davies, MD, insisted that in girls, a narrowing of the waist and slight widening of the hips preceded the formation of breast buds. (In a recent conversation, he added the proviso that this is only true for girls who aren't overweight.) For girls, what comes next is further maturation of the breasts and the development of pubic hair, culminating in menstruation.

I regularly see young adolescent or even preadolescent females whose parents are concerned about lumps felt or seen under one or both of the child's nipples. Parents are usually worried that the lumps are tumors, but they rarely are. This same condition can occur, although less frequently, in boys. A mother recently brought her 11-year-old boy to see me because she was concerned about a tender mass on the left side of the boy's chest that caused him discomfort, particularly when it rubbed against his basketball jersey. I examined him to check for the presence of any other rare conditions that might cause his symptoms and to confirm that there weren't enlarged lymph nodes, which might indicate a more serious problem. There were no indications of a serious condition, and I was able to reassure the mom and to make some suggestions to the boy about how to deal with the discomfort.

For boys, puberty usually begins with enlargement of the testes, the proliferation of pubic hair and the enlargement of the penis into a useful *tool*. Thus, the parents wake up one day to find that their five-foot soprano has transformed into a six-foot baritone. Tremendous growth spurts can occur during puberty, with children growing as much as six or seven inches in a single year, or steadily growing three or four inches per year. This rapid growth often renders the child awkward, as he or she is not yet familiar with this new body and is often tripping over legs that are suddenly too long. It can take several years for a child to gain comfort within his or her new and improved physical structure.

Most adolescent boys think their penises are too small. Once during a hospital lecture on the physiologic changes that occur in puberty, we were shown a cartoon caricature of a boy looking down at his penis. Because of the perspective he was looking at it from, the penis appeared small. From a different angle, everything was well-proportioned, but this distorted view was his frame of reference. For the most part, the situation is similar with girls and their breasts. Consider these body parts equivalent to plumage in birds, meant to attract the other sex, and the preoccupation will start to make more sense.

I'll share one of my secrets with you. As I mentioned earlier, it isn't possible to reliably estimate the ultimate height of a child when he or she is young. But boys are particularly obsessed with their heights, and so I play a game with kids at their 11-or 12-Year Checkups in which I estimate their ultimate adult heights. (I remind them, of course, that I am only making an educated guess.) I make my estimate by looking at their current heights and determining how delayed or advanced they are in sexual development. The more delayed they are, the longer they will grow. Usually I am close in my estimate but occasionally I am way off, particularly when it comes to children who stop growing unexpectedly early in their pubertal stages.

"Joannie," was a neighbor of mine when I was growing up. She went off to seventh grade one day and came home terrified that she was bleeding to death. Her first menstrual cycle had arrived and she was totally unprepared. I'm sure that after the fear receded, she was extremely embarrassed. What ultimate effect this trauma had on Joannie's life, I cannot be sure, but I'd imagine that the experience made traversing this difficult period of life even more troubling for Joannie. Schools usually start teaching kids about sexual development in the fourth or fifth grade, and the hope is that parents have already started discussing bodily changes with their offspring well before the surprise of menstruation. This was not the case when I was growing up.

The Teenage Brain: A Parent's Survival Guide

Not long ago, I received a phone message from a mom regarding her 15-year-old son's upcoming checkup. She was extremely concerned about the boy's recent behavior and wanted to discuss the issue with me in private ahead of our appointment. "Jacob," a previously exemplary child, was now talking back to his parents, had lost interest in some activities and was slacking off slightly in school, where he had previously been an honor student. Mom was also concerned by the fact that the boy had recently attended a party where alcohol — secretly carried in by some of the other juvenile attendees — was present. We arranged to get to the bottom of the situation. During the visit, I spoke to Jacob in private about his recent behavior. He was generally a good kid who was still doing well in school, even if he wasn't quite living up to his full potential. Jacob had good friends and solid interests. His drinking seemed to be a form of experimentation rather than an ongoing issue and he wasn't dabbling in drugs or other risky behaviors. Jacob and I discussed all this, and we talked about why it was important for him to keep working hard in high school. I then invited his mom back into the room. I reassured her that Jacob had no major issues and I told her she needed to back off a bit, barring a serious decrease in her son's school performance.

Along with the great burst of hormones coursing through the adolescent body comes a tendency toward distraction. Girls become moody, while boys' brains migrate below their waists. Some adolescent educators half-jokingly suggest eliminating the seventh and eighth grades and replacing them with some kind of work camps until these surges subside and the brain can once again act reasonably.

Add an adolescent's sense of invincibility and a lack of abstract thinking to the equation, and you have a combination that puts the child at great risk. Some of this can be blamed on the maturing brain. The ability to think abstractly is a process that usually is not complete until mid- or late adolescence, and this ability is essential to understanding the consequences of one's actions. If I steal a car, for example, I know that I may go to jail. Prior to reaching this developmental adolescent milestone, that thought may only occur to me as I am speeding down the highway in my brand new stolen car with the police in hot pursuit.

When my younger son was in high school in the late '90s, two of his classmates attended an unsupervised party and drove home drunk. On the way back, they slammed into an SUV that was carrying a mom and her three young children. Fortunately, the family was fine. Unfortunately, the teenagers were not. One was left permanently brain damaged and was never able to go home. The other classmate had severe head trauma, which took more than a year to resolve. I don't know if he ever completely recovered or if he, too, was left with permanent deficits. Two of my son's other classmates impregnated their girlfriends and became fathers before they'd graduated high school. Their impulsive actions changed the courses of their lives forever.

Adolescents also have a hard time believing that any physical tragedy or illness could befall them. Try telling an adolescent boy that if he continues to smoke he may die of cancer or heart disease. He will look at you as if you are an alien. You are much more likely to get a positive response if you convince him that he will smell and become unattractive to the objects of his romantic inclinations. This feeling of invincibility is important to the ultimate development of independence in the growing child. Conversely, however, serious illness or injury has a much greater impact on the physical and psychological development of an adolescent than it does on a child at most any other age. It's a tricky paradox.

Communication is also essential when it comes to dealing with an adolescent. Even though they pretend they don't hear you, rest assured that they do, so don't be afraid to talk freely about the realities of sex, drugs and alcohol and the dangers of the Internet. Discussing these topics frankly and giving your adolescent information he requests will not lead him to participate in dangerous activities any more than he would have otherwise.

As a parent, you also need to be aware of danger signs in your child's mood and behavior. One of my dictums is that parents should pay less attention to how a child behaves at home and pay more attention to how she performs in school and how she relates to other people. Know who her friends are. It is very reassuring when you get glowing reports about how wonderfully your child behaves and performs in school and when she has nice friends. Know where your children are going and set time limits when they are out at night. Discuss what they think is reasonable and take that into consideration. Teenagers will usually respond better if they are involved in the decision-making process. Set a time when your teenagers need to check in with you, and get a number where they can be reached other than on their own cellphone. Explain to them that you are not asking for these things because you don't trust them but because knowing this information will put you at ease. It's a good idea to call the parents of a friend with whom your child is supposed to visit to make sure there will be parental supervision. Oftentimes when parents are not at home, teenagers have parties at which alcohol and other substances are involved. As discussed above, this can have dangerous consequences.

Parents instinctively want to protect their children. They don't want them to suffer by making mistakes. But everyone makes mistakes. Smart people learn from those mistakes. Less intelligent people repeat them. As Ralph Waldo Emerson said, "Life is a succession of lessons that must be lived to be understood."

This is a very difficult thing for many parents to accept, but it is important to err and occasionally even to fail in order to learn that each mistake doesn't automatically result in disaster. Children who fail to learn this lesson can suffer intensely after they leave the nest. As I was working on this book, I came across a tragic newspaper article about the suicide of a 19-year-old young woman in the next town over from me. Through reading the article and speaking to people who knew her, I gathered that she was the last one anyone would have expected to perform such an act of desperation. In high school, she'd been a great student from a supportive and intact family. She was a top scholar, a star athlete and was pretty and well-liked, and she did it with what seemed like little effort. This girl had it all, and she passed over scholarships to very good colleges to head for the Ivy Leagues. It was there that this formerly "exceptional" young lady found herself suddenly considered only above average. Academically, she was doing well, and she also competed in sports and was pledging a sorority. But doing "well" was a failure in this girl's eyes, as anything less than perfect was simply unacceptable. She'd begun to doubt herself, and despite her parents' suggestions that she transfer to a lower-pressure school, she returned for a second semester. Shortly after that semester started, she jumped to her death.

If you do decide to intervene in your adolescent's life or to punish him for poor decision-making, you should determine specific and *appropriate* consequences that will actually help put him back on track. For the younger teen, an appropriate consequence for bad behavior might be taking away electronics, video games, cell phones or television. For the older teenager, it might be more appropriate to withhold the use of the car. Grounding and limiting extracurricular social activities is also an option. I advise against punishing your child by canceling activities that bring him self-esteem, such as athletics or participation in school plays or musical groups. That should be a last resort.

When misbehavior occurs and a punishment is necessary, it is also best to let everyone's emotions settle before issuing an edict, as it is more likely to be a reasonable one that you are willing and able to carry out. Unlike with a younger child, an adolescent's punishment doesn't have to be instituted immediately after the crime. Idle threats, on the other hand, subvert any credibility and authority that a parent has and encourage future poor behavior.

Reality Check: Helping Your Teen Navigate Sexuality

"Robert" came to see me for his College Checkup. He was a first-generation American and his mother, a domineering professional, rarely left his side. (I never met the dad so I can't comment on his personality type, although I can guess.) At one point during the checkup, this mother and I even had a minor confrontation about whether she should leave the room during the examination to allow him some privacy.

I always try to speak to a patient's parents at some point during the examination, as I want to listen to and address their concerns. Prior to Robert's exam, I discussed recommended immunizations, including the HPV (human papillomavirus) vaccine, which prevents cervical cancer in girls but also prevents other less frequent or serious complications in both males and females. Today, administering the vaccine is the standard of care for this age group. I try to discuss with parents the reasons for giving this vaccine and its possible complications in a manner that is general and doesn't imply any specific sexual activity on the part of the patient. In Robert's case, I explained that he was going off to college, and even if he wasn't currently sexually active, we wanted him to be protected in the event that sex occurred. After all, there's no point closing the barn door after the horses have left. This particular virus can spread through any sort of sexual contact, even if no intercourse occurs.

Robert's mom insisted that he was not ready for sex. She believed that if we vaccinated him, we were basically giving him a license to have sex. Robert demurely suggested that perhaps it was a good idea, to which his mother turned a deaf ear. After I sent Robert's mom out and performed the examination, we discussed the common pitfalls of adolescence, including drugs, alcohol and dangers associated with the Internet, all with the understanding that our discussion was confidential. When the topic turned to sex, Robert disclosed that he had a girlfriend and he proudly admitted that he had gotten to "third base," but he hadn't hit the proverbial home run. (The metaphor indicated that he was playing around sexually but had not yet had intercourse.) In fact, Robert was already potentially at risk for being infected with this virus. The prevalence of HPV in the 14-19 year age group is 35 percent, meaning approximately one in three teenagers in this age group has already been infected. We also discussed protection in the case of sexual penetration to avoid the risk of sexually transmitted infections and pregnancy for the partner. I also reminded Robert and his mom that when a child reaches 18 years of age, he or she is legally entitled to make his or her own decision about this vaccine.

Robert may or may not become intimate with a partner in the near future, but I want to give him and my other patients like him the knowledge they require to avoid potentially life-altering consequences. I do not encourage sexual intercourse in these encounters. I discourage casual sex. I offer the option of celibacy until marriage. For those parents who are invested in denial and self-deception about the risks of adolescent sexual activity, here are some recent numbers: In a 2009 *Youth Risk Behavioral Survey* performed by the Centers for Disease Control and Prevention of students in grades nine through 12, 46 percent of students reported having had sex with at least one person. Of those who hadn't yet had sexual intercourse, 11 percent of girls and 13 percent of boys reported having had heterosexual oral sex.

Sexual preferences also come to the forefront during adolescence. They may, of course, start manifesting themselves earlier, but they only assume importance as the child develops into a physically and emotionally sexual being. The realization that one is sexually attracted to peers of the same sex can be very traumatic. This conflict often causes depression, more often in boys than in girls.

I recently received a call from the mother of one of my adolescent patients, "Brian." I have known Brian's family for more than 20 years. His mom had called me about a different issue but during the call she also informed me that Brian had come out to her as gay several weeks before, acknowledging his sexual orientation to himself, his family and friends. She was not surprised and she was happy that he was very comfortable with himself. She recalled a conversation she'd had with me about Brian's interest in dressing in girl's clothing when he was 5 or 6 years old – a tendency that persisted for a much longer time. As we discussed Brian's coming out, she quoted something I'd told her earlier on: "I have rarely met a child who is happy being forced to be someone he is not."

This advice seemed to make a big difference in her approach to raising her son. Later on in his childhood, when Brian was suffering through an adolescent depression, he saw a therapist who tried to "toughen him up." This didn't go over well. One of the joys of being a pediatrician is to occasionally hear that something you said or did made a significant impact on a patient or family's life. I was thrilled to learn that Brian has recently been accepted to a very prestigious music school for opera.

America is joining nations across the globe in becoming much more tolerant of homosexuality, with the first active professional male athlete, NBA basketball player Jason Collins, recently coming out. Female professional gay athletes have been coming out for much longer. It is generally harder for gay men to gain social acceptance, as the stereotypical image of a gay man is antithetical to the macho image to which most adolescent males aspire. Either way, getting comfortable with your own sexuality is a lot easier when you feel accepted by your parents.

Sometimes a child's sexual identity is far more complex than "gay" or "straight." I first met "Rhianna" born "Ryan" when she was about 10 years of age. Rhianna had been born with ambiguous genitalia, meaning it was unclear whether she was physically male or female. Rhianna was deemed to be a genetic male with a feminizing form of congenital adrenal hyperplasia. In this disease, a block in the production of cortisone and also testosterone occurs, the latter being essential to the formation of the external male genitalia. For treatment, she was sent to Johns Hopkins Medical Center, which was considered the medical Mecca for this type of sexual disorder at the time. Sexual assignments back then were determined solely based on whether the existing sexual organ could adequately function as a penis. In Rhianna's case, a genetic boy with an "inadequate penis" was reconstructed into a physical female. Physically, this reconstruction was much more successful than it would have been had the genitals been altered in the opposite direction. Rhianna was subsequently raised as a girl and treated with female hormones. Unbeknownst to those medical experts, there exists hardwiring in the male DNA that often causes sexual confusion during puberty in these physical "females," many of whom ultimately identify themselves as males. So much for physical attributes being the sole determination of sexual assignment. I don't know what happened to Rhianna. When she graduated from our practice, she was in therapy and was still trying to figure out how to deal with a truly ambiguous situation.

Are Bogeymen Heritable? Supporting Your Adolescent through Tough Times

"Caitlin" was a lovely 17-year-old girl whose parents were divorced. Her father had been caring for her until her mother's recent diagnosis of stage IV colon cancer. Caitlin had moved back in with her mother to help her through the illness, and her relationship with her father was deteriorating. Her schoolwork was also suffering and she was dealing with some eating issues.

Caitlin's dad brought her to see me, as he was very concerned about this turn of events. He wanted to protect his child. He had grown up in China, where his mother had died and the Japanese had killed most of his family. He had been forced to learn survival skills. So he'd immigrated to the United States, joined the military and started a new life. He was a very strong and regimented individual and he wanted to impart these skills to his daughter so she could benefit from his experiences.

As I watched Caitlin twitching during her father's assessment of the situation, I thought about two things at once: dad's good intentions *and* the irrelevance of his childhood experience to his daughter's life. Everything needs to be taken in context. Dad was frustrated by Caitlin's lack of interest, and I explained to him that although the circumstances of his childhood were important and should be shared with Caitlin, they really weren't relevant to her current situation. Parents need to avoid passing on their own bogeymen to their children.

I tried to help Caitlin see that her father had good intentions, and I suggested that they listen to each other in an attempt to develop some mutual understanding. I also explained to both Caitlin and her dad that children of divorce usually take out their anger on the most consistent parent, the one they are least afraid to lose.

I recently also had a visit from two new parents. They were a clean-cut, middle-class couple in their mid-20s, but things hadn't always been this way. The mother was a former heroin user successfully managing her addiction with the use of a synthetic opioid that prevented withdrawal without giving her a high. (This was important to know as it meant we needed to observe the child more closely.) I also spoke to the father, who proudly mentioned that he was a former addict who had been clean for almost a year.

When I asked the father about the origin of his heroin abuse, he explained to me that drug use was pervasive in his high school. He had a group of friends who were bored and had money. They started experimenting with alcohol and marijuana and soon got hooked on prescription pain medications, which could cost $50 a pill. At that point, it became far cheaper to score a $5 bag of heroin. Unfortunately, by the time the two of them found themselves sitting in my office, only two out of the original 15 members of that social group were still alive.

I saw both parents and their new baby shortly afterward, and they were doing well. I also spoke to the social worker at the hospital, who was in contact with both the parents' recovery programs, and I learned that the mom was faithfully attending her weekly meetings and was submitting to scrupulous drug screens. The father was actively participating in a county program through which he received monthly injections designed to cause vomiting if he used narcotics. Having a baby, in and of itself, is not a successful or joyful way to sustain a troubled relationship or to solve one's problems, but I hope that loving each other and having a new precious baby will be enough motivation to keep these two lovely youngsters on the straight and narrow path.

"James" was a 14-year-old patient of mine. He was also a competitive swimmer who had been swimming since age 5. He came to the office complaining of chest pain and concerned that he was having a heart attack. That is a very unusual condition for a child of this age, especially a child with no history of exercise intolerance or fainting. At first I thought it was muscle strain and I treated him with rest and anti-inflammatory medication. Two weeks later I again saw him for the same situation and had an x-ray taken of his chest. The x-ray revealed no signs of lung disease or heart enlargement. I tried to reassure James and his family and I told him to call me if there was still no improvement.

I then asked James whether any situations were causing him anxiety. He denied this possibility. He was a good student and well-liked. His pain persisted and I was forced to do a cardiac evaluation, which came out negative. After I received the results, I saw him for another follow-up, as the pain still hadn't subsided. I reexamined him and then I asked his parents to leave the room.

I then asked James what was really going on.

He tearfully responded: "I don't want to swim."

I suggested to James that we speak to his parents together. I brought them into the room and we discussed this painful situation. They were understanding. James stopped swimming and the pain receded. To be clear, James was not faking his pain. He was physically feeling the heartache he thought he would cause his parents by informing them of his agonizing decision to quit a once-beloved hobby.

I recently saw a very anxious adolescent patient, "Dora." Throughout the exam, she was sitting in a chair in the examination room reading a book. Dora was barely looking up and she responded to all my questions with one-word answers – certainly not one of those patients a physician has to worry about interrupting.

I tried to relate to her by commenting on her love of reading and discussing the contents of the book. She had come in with complaints of congestion, pain and tightness in the chest. Although she had a past history of anxiety disorder, she was convinced she had asthma. However, she was able to participate in all normal activities without a problem.

I reviewed her records and found no past history or family history of asthma, which meant it was unlikely to be the problem. I examined her and noted only mild allergic rhinitis.

When I suggested to Dora that anxiety might be the culprit, her response was extremely strong and antagonistic. She seemed to shut down emotionally even more than she had before. Because Dora seemed offended by my suggestion, I immediately reversed course. I decided instead to suggest that her allergy-related symptoms might be creating some anxiety. She seemed minimally assuaged. The way we phrase our words is extremely important. In this case, it helped to soften a patient with whom the trust relationship was tenuous at best.

Considering the adolescent tendency toward impulsiveness, parents should also scrupulously guard any firearms they decide to keep in the house when teenagers are around. This could prevent a tragic accident or even a self-inflicted injury. In a 2010 review of emergency room visits, it was estimated that there were close to 80,000 child firearm injuries with 114 deaths. Guns were the preferred choice of suicide in the 15- to 19-year-old age group as well as the cause of more than a quarter of all deaths and 85 percent of all homicides in this age group. These rates are 35 times higher in America than they are in any other country.

In light of the recent Columbine, Colorado, and Newtown, Connecticut, school shootings as well as a proliferation of mall and movie theater shootings, I beseech parents not to keep handguns or semiautomatic weapons at home. This is not just my personal recommendation; it's also the recommendation of the American Academy of Pediatrics. A gun is supposed to provide its owner with a means of protection, but in fact guns result in more injuries to innocent people than they do to perpetrators. The safest way to prevent these calamities is to not have these weapons accessible to an age group that is impulsive and sometimes unable to appropriately consider the consequences of actions. The second safest way to prevent accidents and injuries is to store any weapons in the house under lock-and-key.

Never Say "Never," Except When You Should: The Trouble with Absolutes

"Brad" was a 19-and-a-half-year-old college student just finishing his second year of college. He was home for the summer, and he needed a checkup for a summer job. Mom was concerned about the number of illnesses he'd had during his first two years of college. Since starting his sophomore year, Brad had been on antibiotics three times for sinusitis, an ear infection and a prolonged febrile illness. He seemed to be constantly congested, although antibiotic treatments helped somewhat, and his mother suspected that his less-than-optimally-clean living conditions at college were the culprit.

I examined Brad. He was healthy except for an upper respiratory infection, otherwise known as a cold. I explained the most likely scenario to Brad and his mother: Late night college "commitments" and exposure to dust and dust mites along with who knows what else in a boys' fraternity house had run Brad down and tipped the balance in favor of the viruses and bacteria. So often, when worn-down college students return home sick, the most important treatment is rest and tender loving care. Often, a few days at home can be rejuvenating as long as these kids don't continue to burn the candle at both ends.

However, that's not always the case. "Ilanna" was a college student I'd known for about 10 years. I mentioned earlier on an asthmatic patient who was one of the two worst I've encountered in my medical career. Ilanna's sister was the other, and I'd developed a close relationship with her family as a result. Her mom, a nurse, was concerned after her daughter was seen twice in the student health service for enlarged lymph nodes.

Ilanna had been told that this problem was caused by a viral infection, and she came down from college to my office. The feel of her enlarged nodes immediately concerned me. A test for mononucleosis came back negative – usually what you want in a test result, but not in this case. Further testing suggested that Ilanna had Hodgkin's disease, which is a cancer of the white blood cells that forms in the lymph nodes. I referred her to a specialist in pediatric cancer who saw her within 24 hours. She started treatment very soon after, and her doctors wisely arranged to protect her ovaries from future radiation therapy during the subsequent surgery. Ilanna is now in her 40s and she's the mother of two teenage girls. The moral: When you hear hoof beats, you shouldn't necessarily think about zebras. It's important for a pediatrician to consider first the more common and likely possible diagnoses. But if you are in the jungle, what you're hearing might well be a zebra. Ilanna's diagnosis turned out not to be the common one – benign, reactive, enlarged lymph nodes – but the more unlikely one: malignancy, or cancer.

I very recently examined a 10-year-old who came in to the office with abdominal pain and an earache. She also had some inflammation of the tonsils. I told her mom we were going to test for strep throat. Unbeknownst to most people, stomachache is a common symptom of strep throat. Mom asked if fever didn't always accompany strep.

I replied "Not always," just as I'd reply to a parent who questioned a diagnosis of mononucleosis simply because her child was not tired. The ultimate diagnosis for this girl was constipation (the cause of her abdominal pain) and ear pain caused by the eruption of her molars.

There truly are no absolutes. Physicians are dealing with living creatures who usually react in unambiguous ways to specific problems, but there is always a host of variables. Take, for instance, the case of an infection. One must consider the dose and the type of bacteria or viruses involved. There is also the question of how the host (the patient) responds and the condition of his or her immune system. Our immune systems, in turn, are affected by many factors, including nutrition, rest, genetic factors and many more subtle considerations. How the patient responds to a treatment is quite variable and is affected by the choice of antibiotics, the dose, the diligence of administration, the absorption of the antibiotic, the rate at which the body breaks down the antibiotic and the susceptibility of the germ to the antibiotic.

Another axiom I believe in: Never say never! Never say always! At one checkup I performed, after a smarty-pants preadolescent patient made an absolute statement, I responded with the aforementioned dictum.

"Never say 'Never,'" I told her.

"You just said 'Never,'" the girl shot back.

I had no logical answer.

So how does a parent manage to survive a child's adolescence? The first thing you must realize is that in their eyes, you are, ahem, rather stupid. You know nothing. Are you ready for the good news? Just as you've gotten wiser as *you* get older, you'll also get wiser as *they* get older. They will experiment and test you continually. Your job is to give them just enough rope so that they can't hang themselves. You should also take comfort in the knowledge that you've already done most of the hard work. If you've raised your children with plenty of love and limits, they'll emerge from adolescence well-adjusted and ready to tackle the adventure of adulthood.

CONCLUSION

A Final Note on Roots, Wings, and Other Things

AS I CONCLUDED A RECENT TALK to new and expectant parents, I was asked to distill everything I know about raising children into a sentence or two. The first thing that came to my mind was that old axiom: "Parents need to give their children roots to grow with and wings to fly with."

The roots, I explained, are the love, direction and caring you offer your children. That care involves feeding, clothing, and protecting a child, both physically and emotionally. It also means making the child's physical world as safe as possible as well as immunizing him or her to protect against some of the most serious diseases. A parent must also learn to key into a child's emotional needs, holding the child securely when she feels nervous or frightened and reassuring and encouraging her when she is preparing to explore the world. Direction comes in the form of the structure and rules parents lay down as well as the examples they knowingly or unknowingly set.

Preparing a child's wings for flight into early adulthood is just as important, and for some parents, this is the more difficult of the two mandates to successfully execute. This process of letting go starts as early as the time a baby begins to separate from his parents and to establish his first likes and dislikes. This entails both a physical and an emotional separation, each of which requires attention. The infant needs to learn that it is safe to wander away from his parents, within reason, and he should be admonished only when he wanders too far. (I am not a big believer in spanking, but a rare spank on the bottom may be appropriate when a child runs out into the street.) An older child might cull a valuable life lesson from the consequences of staying out past curfew. But it is unacceptable to allow an adolescent to learn such lessons in more reckless ways, such as taking the keys to the car before he has his license.

A growing child also needs to be able to express his ideas and concerns without being constantly shushed or punished for it. Age-appropriate discussions about conflicting wishes, feelings and desires are helpful and educational for children as well as their parents. When you are dealing with a younger child, such debates are necessarily simpler and shorter. When a child becomes able to critically think through a given situation, the pros and cons of opposing viewpoints can be discussed in more detail. It is important for a child to know that he may respectfully disagree with others as long that expression is timed properly and isn't potentially dangerous. (It's certainly not acceptable to threaten to kill a person with whom one disagrees, for example. It's also not appropriate in most contexts to go up to another person and tell them you hate them.)

Your child must also learn to make mistakes and even experience failure sometimes, as long as the situation isn't dangerous and the consequences aren't too severe. Discovering that making mistakes and occasionally failing isn't fatal is critical to building character. Learning from one's mistakes, especially when the results are unpleasant, is an important tool for physical and emotional success later in life.

What's most important of all when it comes to equipping a child with her own set of wings? She must know without a doubt that despite her imperfections, and despite any differences parent and child may have, she is loved. That is the key to feeling secure.

Parenting is a kind of tightrope act: you must constantly strike a balance between setting limits and offering freedom. It is important for parents to realize that they've done most of this foundation-building by the time their child is a teenager. A child's basic character is pretty much set at this stage and all that remains is the fine-tuning. Keep in mind, too, that the finished product (the adult) is only partially the result of parenting. The rest is the result of genetic factors that you pass on but cannot much control, such as temperament and intelligence. Parents need to reinforce their children's strengths and to help them overcome their weaknesses while avoiding either coddling or constant criticism. And remember: If you are willing to take the blame for your child's deficiencies, you should be equally willing to accept the praise for that child's good characteristics. The children you leave behind you will make up your lasting legacy on earth, so don't forget to stop occasionally to admire your handiwork.

Yes, parenting is trying! Children can certainly create stress in your marriage and personal life, and things will absolutely never be the same, so be sure and take time to enjoy the simple pleasures this journey affords. Embrace the excitement your child experiences with each new day and each new situation. Open yourself up to the wonder of childhood. You'll be exposed to new ideas and to new ways of thinking, and you'll benefit from your proximity to the undeniable energy of youth.

Parenting is a difficult endeavor, but it's also an immensely rewarding one. A grand adventure, indeed.

I hope you enjoy the trip.

37908199R00107

Made in the USA
Charleston, SC
25 January 2015